MW01119173

The Only Estate Planning Book You'll Ever Need

How to Organize Your Assets, Protect Your
Loved Ones, Save Thousands on Legal Fees
& Find the Right Lawyer
(+ Handle Wills and Trusts)

By

Garrett Monroe

This publication is designed to provide accurate and authoritative information in regard to the subject matter covered. The advice and strategies contained herein may not be suitable for your situation. You should consult with a professional when appropriate. Neither the publisher nor the author shall be liable for any loss of profit or any other commercial damages, including but not limited to special, incidental, consequential, personal, or other damages.

Buyer Bonus

As a way of saying thank you for your purchase, we're offering two FREE downloads that are exclusive to our book readers!

First, the Estate Planning Checklist which shows you a step-by-step guide to getting your estate plan in order. Second, the Legacy Planning Workbook, which provides a roadmap for preserving your legacy and leaving a lasting impact on future generations. Inside these bonuses, **you'll discover:**

- An exact checklist for each phase of the estate planning process, so you leave no stone unturned and make sure you're fully prepared.

- A blueprint for sharing your values and having important conversations with heirs about your estate plan, so your wishes are properly fulfilled.

- The 6 key things you MUST have in order to properly preserve your legacy and leave your heirs protected.

To download your bonuses, you can go to **MonroeMethod.com/estate-plan or simply scan the QR code below:**

Contents

The Power of Estate Planning

As the old saying goes, "The best time to plant a tree was 20 years ago. The second best time is now." This wisdom rings *especially* true when it comes to planning for your future. Often wrapped in misconceptions of requiring vast wealth or the foresight of a financial guru, estate planning is a fundamental step for anyone looking to secure their legacy and provide for their loved ones. It isn't just about dividing assets—it's also about imparting a piece of yourself and your hard-earned life's work to future generations. It's about making decisions today that'll protect and guide those you care about the most long after you're gone.

Whether you're just starting to build your life's foundation or reflecting on the legacy you wish to leave behind, estate planning is important in ensuring that your wishes are honored. Let's embark on this journey together and make it accessible to *everyone*—not just the rich and famous. It's time to plant your tree, and there's no better moment than now.

The Keystone of Legacy Planning: Why Your Story Matters

Estate planning is essential in securing your financial legacy and ensuring peace of mind for your loved ones. This process is more than asset distribution—it's also an act of foresight that safeguards your life's achievements and the well-being of those you hold dear. It isn't a luxury reserved for the affluent but rather a fundamental right and responsibility for everyone.

Through thoughtful planning, you can navigate the complexities of laws and taxes, prevent potential family disputes, and uphold your wishes with dignity and precision. The thesis of this book posits that effective estate planning is something that everyone should do with their finances, serving as a bridge between present intentions and future realities. By embracing estate planning, people of all backgrounds can leave a legacy that reflects their values, supports their loved ones, and stands the test of time.

Unlocking the Power of Your Legacy: The Why & How of Estate Planning

The primary purpose of this book is to examine the often complex and misunderstood process of estate planning and to ensure that it's accessible and understandable for everyone. Estate planning is filled with legal jargon and complex laws that vary from one jurisdiction to another. We'll simplify these concepts and break down the barriers that might otherwise prevent you from taking the steps to protect your legacy.

You'll be guided by practical advice, real-life examples, and actionable steps to navigate the process of drafting wills, setting up trusts, and understanding the implications of your choices.

What We'll Be Covering

The following is a brief overview of what each chapter offers:

Chapter 1: Getting the Big Picture on Estate Planning

This chapter introduces estate planning and demonstrates its importance for everyone—not just the wealthy. It busts common myths and highlights why estate planning is crucial to personal financial management.

Chapter 2: The Complete Guide to Organizing Your Assets

Learn how to inventory your assets, understand common titling mistakes, and identify everything you own. You'll be provided with detailed advice on valuing your intangible assets and organizing your financial information for easy access and management.

Chapter 3: Protecting Your Loved Ones Through Estate Planning

Focusing on family, this chapter explores how to use trusts, wills, and other estate-planning tools to provide for your significant other, children, and other beneficiaries. It covers guardianship considerations, survivorship rights, and planning for long-term care, alongside strategies to minimize family disputes and ensure that your wishes are carried out.

Chapter 4: DIY Estate Planning & Choosing The Right Lawyer

Navigate the balance between DIY estate planning and the need for professional legal advice. We'll explore when to consider DIY options, the risks involved, and how to effectively choose and work with the right lawyer to ensure that your estate planning meets your needs.

Chapter 5: The Great Debate Between Wills & Trusts

You'll discover the differences between wills and trusts, their advantages and disadvantages, and how to decide which is right for your situation. Real-life scenarios help illustrate the impact of each choice on estate-planning goals.

Chapter 6: Live Long & Prosper: Planning for Your Retirement

Connect the dots between estate planning and retirement planning. This chapter covers how to leverage your retirement accounts, understand healthcare costs, and use estate planning to secure your financial future in retirement.

Chapter 7: Brace Yourself - Estate Taxes Are Coming

Gain an understanding of estate and inheritance taxes and learn strategies to minimize your tax liability. We'll examine how gifting, trusts, and charitable bequests can reduce your estate's tax exposure.

Chapter 8: When Life Changes, Update Your Estate Plan

We'll address how life events like marriage, divorce, and the birth of children should trigger a review of your estate plan, and provide you with tips on how to keep your plan current regardless of any changes in your life.

Chapter 9: Probate - Keeping Calm & Carrying On

Understand the probate process, as well as how to avoid and navigate it if necessary. This chapter offers a step-by-step guide through probate and how to manage disputes should they arise.

Chapter 10: Seize the Day - Taking Control of Your Estate Plan Now

Our closing chapter encourages you to take action on your estate planning with practical steps to get started. You'll learn how to overcome procrastination and gain the peace of mind that comes with having a plan in place.

What Not to Do

When it comes to estate planning, a few common missteps can lead to headaches and heartaches for both you and your loved ones. First of all, let's cast aside the opinion that estate planning is only for the wealthy. In fact, it's essential for anyone who wants to have a say in how their assets are handled and their wishes honored.

Avoid the trap of "set it and forget it." Life changes, and so should your estate plan. Ignoring the need to update your documents can render them as useful as an expired coupon. Also, don't *ever* go at it alone with a DIY will from the internet without consulting a professional. While saving a few bucks is always tempting, this approach can cost you and your heirs significantly more in the long run.

You, the Legacy Maker: Charting the Path Forward

Take a moment to answer this question honestly: How often do you think about the legacy you're going to leave behind? Maybe it's something that crosses your mind every now and then, or maybe it's a thought that you quickly brush away (an all-too-common reaction). But let's imagine, just for a second, what your ideal legacy would look like. Would it be ensuring your family's financial security? Supporting a cause that's close to your heart? Or maybe just making sure that your loved ones aren't left with a mess to sort out after you're gone?

Whatever your vision, estate planning is the tool that can make it a reality. Think of this book as your friendly guide through what might otherwise seem like a maze of legalities and decisions. We're here to break it down, keep it simple, and maybe even have a bit of fun along the way. So let's dive in and explore how you can craft an estate plan that reflects your wishes, cares for your loved ones, and secures your legacy.

Before We Get Started

You might have found yourself wondering, "Who is this Garrett Monroe, and what insights does he have regarding estate planning? How qualified is this guy?"

It's a valid comment. After all, entrusting your legacy and planning intricacies requires more than just a leap of faith—it also demands confidence in the guide you choose to follow.

Garrett Monroe isn't a single expert but rather a consortium of knowledge and experience—a pen name for a diverse team of writers, each with a rich background in various sectors including estate planning, retirement strategies, accounting, and more. This collective has navigated industries like estate planning and trusts, coaching, sales, and entrepreneurship, accumulating a wealth of understanding on managing people, building successful teams, and crafting a fulfilling life.

Together, under the banner of Garrett Monroe, these writers have converged their expertise to offer you a comprehensive guide through the often tangled web of estate planning. Their shared goal? To elevate your financial acumen, business endeavors, and overall contentment to unprecedented heights.

So as we proceed, rest assured that the insights and strategies shared are drawn from a wellspring of real-world experience and collective wisdom tailored to help you secure your legacy with confidence and clarity.

Chapter 1

Getting the Big Picture on Estate Planning

"A man who does not plan long ahead will find trouble at his door."
-Confucius, Chinese Philosopher

Estate Planning: Not Just for the Rich and Famous

Why Everyone Needs Estate Planning (Even You)

As mentioned earlier, estate planning often carries the misconception that it's a luxury suited only for the affluent or older people. However, the truth is starkly different and far more inclusive. Estate planning is an undertaking for everyone, regardless of wealth, age, or status. It's about taking control of your future, ensuring that your wishes are honored, and protecting those you love after you leave.

The benefits of having a plan in place are universal. First, it provides clarity and direction for the distribution of your assets, no matter how modest or extensive they may be. This means less stress and uncertainty for your loved ones during a difficult time. Second, it allows you to appoint guardians for your children, ensuring that they're cared for by people you trust and in the way you want. Third, estate planning is about minimizing the burden on your family. It can reduce the expenses and delays associated with probate, the legal process of distributing your estate (which can be both time consuming and costly).

Think of it this way: Estate planning is an act of thoughtfulness and responsibility. It's about making selfless decisions today to protect and provide for your loved ones tomorrow. Regardless of your current financial situation or stage in life, estate planning is a powerful tool that affords you peace of mind, knowing that your wishes are documented and your family's future is secure.

Busting the Myths About Estate Planning

"Estate planning" – just hearing the words can conjure up some misconceptions to deter people from taking the necessary steps to secure their legacy. Let's debunk some of these common inaccuracies and set the record straight.

First, the myth that estate planning is only for the wealthy couldn't be further from the truth. Regardless of the size of your estate, planning can ensure that your assets are distributed according to your wishes and not the default laws of your state. It's about making sure that your hard-earned assets benefit your loved ones.

Another myth is that estate planning is only for older people. In reality, it's about preparing for the unexpected, and life's uncertainties definitely don't discriminate by age. Young adults, especially those with dependents or assets, must consider how their responsibilities will be managed should anything happen to them.

Lastly, many believe that estate planning is too complex and overwhelming. While the thought of dealing with legal documents (not to mention the idea of dying) isn't exactly thrilling, the process becomes much more manageable with the right guidance. Today, resources and professionals can help simplify the process, making estate planning accessible to everyone.

Debunking these myths opens the door to understanding estate planning as an inclusive, necessary step for anyone interested in protecting their assets and providing for their loved ones. It's a proactive measure, not a reaction to aging or wealth accumulation, and it's much simpler to execute than many believe.

Practical Benefits: How Estate Planning Helps Beyond Wealth Preservation

Estate planning serves multiple practical benefits that touch on every facet of personal and financial well-being. One huge advantage is avoiding probate, which is the often lengthy and costly court process required to distribute assets if you die intestate (i.e., without a will). By having a solid estate plan that includes a will or a trust, you can streamline the distribution of your assets, ensuring that they go directly to your beneficiaries without unnecessary delay or public scrutiny.

Estate planning empowers you to ensure that your wishes are respected. Through documents like a will, you're able to dictate who receives your assets, while a living will and durable power of attorney for healthcare decisions ensure that your wishes regarding medical treatment are followed if you can't communicate. This level of control is impossible without proper planning.

Protecting your family's future is another facet of estate planning. It's about safeguarding your loved ones from the unexpected, and it extends far greater than merely distributing your assets. For families with young children, an estate plan can appoint guardians, avoiding the possibility of state intervention in custody matters. Additionally, it can provide for any special needs your family members may have, ensuring that they're cared for in your absence.

Celebrity Estate Blunders: Lessons to Learn From

Celebrity estate blunders offer us cautionary tales about the importance of diligent estate planning. For instance, legendary musician Prince died without a will, leading to a complex and public legal battle. His estate, valued at over $200 million, took over six years to settle, underscoring the chaos that ensues when one's wishes aren't legally documented.

Similarly, despite her substantial assets, Aretha Franklin's passing revealed that she had no formal will. Handwritten notes discovered in her home sparked disputes among her children, highlighting how even informal attempts at outlining one's wishes can lead to confusion and conflict without proper legal structure.

James Gandolfini, star of "The Sopranos," did have an estate plan but was heavily criticized for its lack of tax planning. The bulk of his $70 million estate was subjected to taxes, significantly diminishing the inheritance for his heirs. Comprehensive planning should always include considerations for tax implications to protect your estate's value.

And Heath Ledger's outdated will unfortunately left nothing to his daughter Matilda, since it was created before her birth. This oversight resulted in family interventions to ensure that she was provided for, whereas if he'd updated it as life unfolded, it would've been a much smoother process.

These examples highlight the critical consequences of neglecting estate planning or failing to prepare adequately. They're powerful reminders that without a clear, legally sound plan, your estate can become mired in costly legal disputes and diminish in value rather than serving as a legacy for your loved ones.

Why Start Now: The Importance of Early Estate Planning

Financial Perks of Early Planning

Estate planning early in life offers financial perks that can enhance the value of your estate and maximize the benefits for your heirs. One of the key advantages is the potential for tax savings. By utilizing trusts and other estate-planning tools, you can minimize exposure to estate and inheritance taxes, ensuring that a larger portion of your assets goes directly to your beneficiaries rather than to tax payments.

Another financial benefit is the power of compound interest. Starting early for assets placed in investment vehicles or trusts allows more time for these investments to grow, and this compounding effect can significantly increase the value of your estate over time. Albert Einstein is famously quoted as saying, "Compound interest is the eighth wonder of the world. He who understands it, earns it…he who doesn't…pays it."

Early planning also allows for more strategic asset distribution. It permits you to thoughtfully consider how and when your assets should be distributed to align with your goals, such as providing for a child's education or supporting a partner. Additionally, you can structure your estate to offer staggered inheritances or set up trusts that protect your assets from beneficiaries' creditors, ensuring that your wealth serves your intended purpose over the long term.

Starting your estate planning journey early secures your financial legacy and gives you the peace of mind that comes from knowing that your affairs are in order, your loved ones are provided for, and your wishes will be honored.

Emotional Perks: How Early Planning Eases Future Worries

Estate planning well ahead of time offers emotional benefits that resonate deeply with both you and your loved ones. The comfort that comes from having an estate plan in place is invaluable. Knowing that your wishes are documented and your affairs are in order can reduce stress and anxiety about the future, both for yourself and those you care about.

This preemptive step ensures that your family won't be left guessing about your desires during a time of grief. It eliminates potential disputes over assets or decisions, which can often drive wedges between family members. Instead, your clear directives can bring unity and understanding, providing your loved ones with a roadmap during an emotionally turbulent time.

Moreover, early estate planning allows for open conversations with your family about your wishes and your reasons for them. These discussions can be incredibly meaningful, offering all involved a sense of closure and preparedness. They also provide an opportunity to address any concerns or questions your loved ones may have, ensuring that everyone is on the same page.

Ultimately, the emotional perks of early estate planning lie in knowing that you've done all you can to protect and provide for your loved ones' future. This foresight eases your mind and serves as a final act of love and consideration, leaving a legacy of thoughtfulness and care.

Resilience Perks: Being Prepared for Unexpected Life Events

Life is fraught with unexpected events, be it sudden illness, accidents, or untimely death. Without a plan in place, these situations can leave your family in a precarious position, both emotionally and financially. Early estate planning is a buffer, ensuring that your loved ones are protected and can maintain their standard of living despite unforeseen challenges.

Getting your affairs in order early allows for durable powers of attorney and healthcare directives. These tools ensure that if you're incapacitated, someone you trust can make financial and medical decisions on your behalf that align with your wishes. This precautionary measure prevents a scramble for control in emergencies and provides a clear directive when making decisions at a time when it's most difficult.

An early-established estate plan can also safeguard your family's financial future. It ensures that assets are transferred smoothly to your beneficiaries, avoiding the delays and expenses associated with probate. This transition can help during times of unexpected hardship and provide immediate financial support to cover living expenses, medical bills, or funeral costs. Countless people don't have a plan in place and then an accident happens, leaving loved ones with an unimaginable stressful situation. Not only must they deal with the death of a loved one but they're also unable to access the family's wealth.

Lastly, early estate planning fosters a sense of security. Knowing that a plan is in place to protect your interests in any circumstance can offer emotional support, reducing stress and anxiety during already challenging times. This preparedness underscores your commitment to your family's well-being, reinforcing the bonds of trust and care.

Simplicity Perks: Why It's Easier When You Start Early

Starting the estate-planning process early simplifies what can otherwise be more challenging. It means that you're not under any pressure from looming health issues or the natural stresses of advanced age, allowing you to approach the process with a clear mind and the time to consider your options thoroughly. This head start grants you the luxury of reflection, enabling you to make decisions that truly reflect your wishes and values.

Moreover, beginning early offers the opportunity to build your plan gradually. Estate planning needs to evolve as your life changes. Starting the process when you're younger allows you to make incremental adjustments as your circumstances shift—be it through marriage, the birth of children, or the acquisition of significant assets. This adaptability ensures that your estate plan remains aligned with your current situation and future goals without rushing last-minute changes.

An early start also helps you understand the estate planning process. By educating yourself on the different aspects of estate planning, including wills, trusts, healthcare directives, and powers of attorney, you become more comfortable with these concepts, making the process less complex and intimidating. This familiarity encourages more informed and confident decision making.

The simplicity perk of starting your estate planning journey early transforms a potentially stressful process into a manageable and even empowering process. It ensures that your legacy is crafted exactly as you envision, with ample room for thoughtful consideration and peace of mind.

Understanding the Basics of Wills, Trusts & Estates

Key Legal Terms To Know

Understanding the language of estate planning can help, **so the following are some key legal terms to know:**

- **Will:** A legal document outlining how a person's assets should be distributed upon death. It can also appoint a guardian for minor children.

- **Trust[1]:** A fiduciary arrangement allowing a third party (i.e., trustee) to hold assets on behalf of a beneficiary or beneficiaries. Trusts can be arranged in many ways and can specify exactly how and when the assets pass to the beneficiaries.

- **Executor:** The individual appointed in a will to manage the estate. This person will execute the will's instructions under the supervision of the probate court.

- **Probate:** The legal process through which a deceased person's will is validated and their estate settled, including the distribution of assets to beneficiaries, payment of debts, and sale of property.

- **Beneficiary:** A person or entity designated to receive assets from a will, trust, insurance policy, or other financial instrument.

- **Power of Attorney:** A legal document that grants an individual the authority to act on another person's behalf in legal or financial matters.

---

[1] https://www.investopedia.com/terms/t/trust.asp

- **Guardianship:** A legal process by which someone is appointed to manage a minor or incapacitated person's personal and/or financial affairs.

- **Estate Tax:** A tax levied on an individual's estate after their death based on the value of their assets.

- **Trustee:** An individual or institution appointed to manage trust assets according to the trust document's terms.

- **Intestate:** Dying without a will, which means that state laws will determine how the deceased's assets are distributed.

There are many terms to know, but these are a great start with which to build your knowledge base.

The Anatomy of a Will: Essential Elements & Functions

A will is the starting point in estate planning, a personal declaration of your wishes regarding the distribution of your assets after your death. Its purpose is to ensure that your estate is handled according to your preferences, not left to your state's default laws of intestacy, which decide asset distribution in the absence of a will.

The components of a will include:

- **Declaration:** The document must clearly state that it's your will and express your intention to dispose of your assets posthumously.

- **Executor Appointment:** Naming an executor, the person you trust to carry out the instructions in your will, is another step. This individual manages your estate, from paying off debts to distributing assets to your beneficiaries.

- **Beneficiaries Identification:** Your will should clearly identify your beneficiaries—the people or organizations you wish to inherit your assets. You can specify what each beneficiary is to receive, whether specific items, amounts of money, or percentages of your estate.

- **Guardianship for Minors:** If you have dependent children, your will can specify who you wish to appoint as their guardian, ensuring that they're cared for by someone you trust in your absence.

- **Signatures:** For a will to be legally valid, it must be signed by you and, typically, at least two witnesses who are not beneficiaries.

Incorporating these elements into your will means that your assets are distributed as you desire, offering assurance that your legacy will be honored. Without a will, you leave the fate of your estate—and potentially the well-being of your loved ones—to chance and legal proceedings, which can be both time consuming and costly.

Different Types of Trusts Explained

Trusts are versatile tools in estate planning offering various benefits, from tax savings to privacy and avoiding probate. Understanding the different types of trusts can help you decide how they might fit into your estate plan, either complementing your will or serving as a standalone solution for certain assets. Be sure to contact an expert before setting these up, as doing so improperly can lead to headaches and financial consequences.

To navigate estate planning effectively, familiarize yourself with the various types of trusts available. Each caters to specific needs and objectives, providing a tailored asset management and protection approach. **Below are the most common:**

1. **Revocable Living Trust:** This flexible trust allows you to maintain control over your assets during your lifetime, with the ability to alter or revoke the trust as your circumstances change. Upon your death, assets in the trust bypass probate and are distributed directly to beneficiaries according to your instructions.

2. **Irrevocable Trust:** Once established, this trust can't be easily altered or revoked. It offers significant tax benefits and asset protection, as assets placed in the trust are removed from your taxable estate. This type of trust is often used for life insurance policies (irrevocable life insurance trust) or to protect assets from creditors.

3. **Charitable Trust:** Designed for philanthropic purposes, charitable trusts can provide tax benefits while allowing you to contribute to charitable organizations either during your lifetime (charitable lead trust) or after your death (charitable remainder trust).

4. **Special Needs Trust:** This trust is established to benefit a person with disabilities, allowing them to receive inheritance or gifts without affecting their eligibility for government assistance programs.

5. **Spendthrift Trust:** Protects the beneficiary's inheritance from their own potential recklessness, creditors, or legal judgments by controlling the distribution of assets.

Each type of trust serves a specific purpose and addresses different aspects of estate planning, from asset protection and tax planning to providing for a loved one with special needs. By integrating trusts into your estate plan, you can achieve greater control and flexibility over managing and distributing your assets.

What Constitutes Your Estate (& What Doesn't)

Generally, your estate includes all assets you own at the time of your death, **but nuances do exist regarding what's included and what isn't:**

Included in Your Estate:

1. **Real Property:** This includes homes, rental properties, and land.

2. **Personal Property:** Cars, furniture, jewelry, and other personal items fall into this category.

3. **Financial Accounts:** Bank, investment, and retirement accounts, though some of these may pass directly to named beneficiaries outside of the probate process.

4. **Life Insurance Policies:** Proceeds from your own life insurance policies are included in your estate for tax purposes, even if the benefits are paid directly to beneficiaries.

5. **Business Interests:** Ownership in businesses and partnerships.

Common Misconceptions:

- **Jointly Owned Property:** While jointly owned property with the right of survivorship typically passes directly to the co-owner and not through your estate, you should still understand how different forms of joint ownership can affect your estate.

- **Retirement Accounts and Life Insurance:** Accounts and policies with named beneficiaries (like IRAs, 401(k)s, and life insurance policies) generally bypass your will and aren't considered part of your estate for probate purposes, though they may still be included for estate tax calculations.

- **Trust Assets:** Assets held in a trust aren't owned by you personally, and thus aren't included in your estate for probate purposes.

Clarifying these distinctions ensures that your estate plan accurately reflects your intentions and provides for your loved ones as you intend, minimizing the potential for confusion and disputes after your death.

The Critical Role of Estate Planning in Asset Protection

Preventing Unnecessary Asset Loss

Estate planning is a strategic process designed to protect your assets from unnecessary loss. The following are some key strategies to mitigate loss through taxes, **probate, and mismanagement:**

1. **Avoiding Probate:** Probate can be time consuming and expensive, eating into the assets you intend to leave behind. By creating a living trust, you can transfer assets to your beneficiaries without going through probate, saving you time and money. Designating beneficiaries on accounts such as life insurance policies and retirement accounts can also bypass probate entirely.

2. **Tax Planning:** Estate taxes can significantly diminish what your heirs receive. Strategies like gifting during your lifetime can reduce the size of your taxable estate since gifts up to a certain annual limit per recipient ($15,000 in 2021) aren't subject to gift tax. Establishing trusts, such as irrevocable life insurance trusts, can also remove assets from your estate, reducing potential estate taxes.

3. **Asset Protection:** Consider forming asset protection trusts to safeguard assets from creditors and legal judgments. These trusts can provide a secure haven for your assets, ensuring that they're preserved for your beneficiaries.

4. **Minimizing Mismanagement:** Selecting a trustworthy and competent executor or trustee can prevent mismanagement of your estate. This individual will manage your estate according to your wishes, so make sure that you choose someone with the right skills and integrity.

Implementing these estate planning strategies can significantly reduce the risk of asset loss due to taxes, probate, and mismanagement, ensuring that your legacy is preserved and protected for future generations.

Family Feuds: How Estate Planning Can Minimize Disputes

A well-crafted estate plan can help minimize the potential for family feuds over inheritance. Clear, detailed instructions on asset distribution can prevent misunderstandings and disputes among heirs, ensuring that your wishes are carried out smoothly and reducing the emotional strain on your loved ones during an already trying time.

One key strategy is openly communicating your estate plan with family members. While it might seem challenging to discuss these matters, transparency can alleviate potential tensions by clarifying your intentions and the reasoning behind your decisions. This preemptive step allows for questions and concerns to be addressed directly, reducing the likelihood of surprises or grievances after your passing.

Incorporating a no-contest clause in your will or trust is another effective measure. This discourages disputes by stipulating that anyone who challenges the estate plan risks losing their inheritance. While not foolproof or enforceable in all jurisdictions, it can be a strong deterrent against litigation.

Equally important is ensuring equitable treatment of heirs. While "equal" doesn't always mean "the same," providing for heirs in a manner perceived as fair can reduce resentment. If certain disparities are necessary, explaining the rationale in your estate documents or a separate letter can help mitigate potential conflicts.

Lastly, regularly updating your estate plan to reflect changes in your family dynamics, such as marriages, divorces, and births, ensures that your estate plan remains relevant and fair, further minimizing the potential for disputes. Taking these steps can create a legacy of harmony, not conflict, for your family.

Creditors & Lawsuits: Shielding Your Assets Through Estate Planning

Proper estate planning offers a strong shield against creditors, lawsuits, and other financial threats, safeguarding your assets for the benefit of your heirs. Implementing strategic measures can ensure that your hard-earned wealth is protected and passed on as you intend rather than by legal claims.

One effective strategy is using **irrevocable trusts**. Unlike revocable trusts, which can be altered or rescinded by the grantor, these are generally beyond the reach of creditors once assets have been transferred into them. The assets in these trusts are no longer considered part of your personal estate, thus protecting them from claims. However, establish these trusts well before any legal threats arise and with expert help, as transfers made with the intent to defraud creditors can be challenged and reversed.

Asset protection trusts, specifically designed to shield assets from creditors, can be another line of defense. These must be carefully structured according to state laws, which vary in their provisions for such protections.

Homestead exemptions are also vital to consider. Many states offer protections for your primary residence, safeguarding a portion or, in some cases, the entirety of your home's value from creditors.

Finally, purchasing **umbrella insurance** can provide additional protection against lawsuits, covering liabilities beyond the limits of standard insurance policies.

You can protect your assets from potential financial threats by integrating some or all of these strategies into your estate plan.

The Role of Insurance in Protecting Your Assets

In estate planning and asset protection, insurance can be your friend, safeguarding your estate's financial health and the well-being of your heirs. Life insurance, long-term care insurance, and other forms of coverage provide a financial safety net, ensuring that your planning objectives are met even in the face of unforeseen circumstances.

- **Life insurance** offers a straightforward solution for creating immediate liquidity upon death. It can pay off debts, cover estate taxes, and provide for your dependents, ensuring that your other assets aren't prematurely liquidated under unfavorable conditions. Furthermore, the proceeds from a life insurance policy are typically paid out quickly and directly to beneficiaries, bypassing probate and potentially estate taxes when properly structured, such as through an irrevocable life insurance trust.

- **Long-term care insurance** addresses a different but equally important concern: the risk of depleting your estate due to the high costs of long-term care. By covering the expenses associated with extended healthcare needs, this insurance preserves your estate for your intended beneficiaries rather than being consumed by medical costs.

- **Disability insurance** is another key strategy, providing income replacement in the event that you're unable to work due to disability. This ensures that your financial plans remain on track, protecting your assets and your family's lifestyle during difficult times.

Incorporating these insurance strategies into your estate plan protects your assets and secures a financial legacy for your heirs. Through careful planning and the strategic use of insurance, you can shield your estate from significant financial threats.

Key Takeaways

- **Universal Necessity:** Estate planning is essential for everyone, not just the wealthy or elderly. It ensures that your wishes are honored and your loved ones protected.

- **Debunking Myths:** It's a common misconception that estate planning is overly complex or only for the affluent. In reality, however, it's accessible for all.

- **Avoiding Probate:** A well-structured estate plan helps bypass the time-consuming and costly probate process, directly benefiting your heirs.

- **Protecting Your Family's Future:** Beyond asset distribution, estate planning secures guardianship for minors and provisions for family members with special needs.

- **The Importance of Early Planning:** Starting the estate planning process early offers significant advantages, including financial benefits and peace of mind.

- **Learning from Mistakes:** Celebrity estate planning failures highlight the importance of having a clear, legally sound plan to avoid disputes and preserve your legacy.

Chapter 2

The Complete Guide to Organizing Your Assets

Creating Your Inventory: Listing What You Own

When starting your estate plan, first thing's first: You need to know what you own. It's like taking stock of everything in your life that has value—not just to make a list but also to make sure that everything you've worked hard for goes exactly where you want it to when you're not around. It's about giving yourself and the people who might be sorting things out later a clear picture of what's what.

This brings us to the matter of titling. If you've ever wondered who really owns what, that's where titling comes in, which is essentially about whose name is on the paperwork. Whether it's your house, your car, or your retirement fund, how these things are titled can make a big difference. It decides if your assets will have to wait around in probate court or if this can be overstepped, ensuring that your assets go straight to the people you've named in your estate. Making sure that everything's titled correctly means that there's no guesswork about who gets what later on.

As we kick off this inventory of your assets, keep in mind that it's more than just making a list. It's about making sure that every item you own is lined up with your plans—clear and simple. No fancy words, just straight-up planning to make sure that your possessions and property end up in the right hands.

Common Asset Titling Mistakes

A common error in estate planning is the incorrect titling of assets, which can affect asset distribution and the finalization of an estate plan. This often occurs with joint titling between non-spouses, which might be intended for convenience but can lead to the asset passing directly to the co-owner, regardless of the decedent's wishes expressed in their will. This can disrupt inheritance plans, particularly if the asset is to be divided among several heirs.

Another frequent mistake is neglecting to designate or update beneficiary designations on retirement accounts, insurance policies, and other accounts that transfer upon death. Outdated beneficiary information can lead to assets being distributed to an ex-spouse or estranged family members, contrary to the deceased's current wishes.

Additionally, failing to title assets in the name of a trust is a missed opportunity for those who've taken the step to create a trust for estate-planning purposes. This oversight means that those assets must go through probate, negating one of the primary benefits of having a trust, which is to avoid probate and ensure privacy and efficiency in asset distribution.

Correctly titling assets ensures that your estate plan works as intended. It's a detail-oriented process that requires regular review and updates to align with your current wishes and life circumstances so that your assets are distributed according to your plans.

Show Me the Money: Identifying Your Assets

This is the first step in comprehensive estate planning. Beyond the obvious (real estate, bank accounts, and investment portfolios), you need to recognize and catalog frequently overlooked assets that can be of significant value. Digital assets, for instance, encompass everything from online banking and brokerage accounts to social media profiles and cryptocurrency. Given their increasing value and complexity, ensuring that they're accounted for and accessible to heirs is necessary.

Collectibles and personal items such as art, jewelry, antiques, and even rare books often carry both sentimental and monetary value, making their identification and valuation important for your estate. Similarly, minor investments such as shares in small businesses or crowdfunding ventures can add up and should never be overlooked.

The failure to identify and list these assets can lead to complications in the estate settlement process, potentially leaving valuable assets unclaimed or causing disputes among heirs. A thorough inventory ensures that every piece of your estate is recognized and properly managed, reflecting your full legacy and simplifying the distribution process for your executors and beneficiaries.

Getting Specific: The Importance of Inventory Details

The specificity of your asset inventory can help with a seamless estate-planning process. Detailed information including account numbers, locations of physical assets, and access information for digital assets not only simplifies the executor's job but also ensures that your assets are accurately identified and distributed according to your wishes. For financial accounts like banking, investment, and retirement accounts, precise account numbers and the institutions where they're held can help avoid confusion and delays in asset distribution.

Physical assets such as real estate, vehicles, and valuable personal items require clear descriptions and locations. This detail prevents any ambiguity that could lead to disputes among beneficiaries. Additionally, you should specify the location and how to access assets in safety deposit boxes or storage units.

Digital assets present unique challenges, often requiring passwords or encryption keys for access. Leaving detailed instructions on how to access these digital assets such as social media accounts, digital wallets, and online accounts is something you absolutely need to do. Without this information, valuable or sentimental digital assets could be lost forever.

Essentially, the more detailed your inventory, the smoother the estate administration process. It's not just about what you own but also centers around providing the clear, actionable information needed to honor your legacy as intended.

What's In The Box? Classifying Your Assets

Classifying your assets into distinct categories is a step that can streamline both management and valuation. Typically, assets can be grouped into key classes: real estate, personal property, investments, digital assets, and collectibles.

- **Real estate** includes primary residences, vacation homes, rental properties, and any other land or buildings you own. This category identifies some of your estate's substantial value and potential tax implications.

- **Personal property** encompasses tangible items like vehicles, furniture, jewelry, and artwork. These items often have both monetary and sentimental value, requiring careful consideration in estate distribution.

- **Investments** cover a broad range, from stocks and bonds to mutual funds and retirement accounts. These assets are used to determine your estate's financial health and plan for future growth or income needs.

- **Digital assets** are increasingly important and include online bank accounts, cryptocurrency, social media profiles, and digital copyrights. Their management and transfer require specific instructions due to their intangible nature.

- **Collectibles** such as antiques, stamps, or rare books might have significant value and special interest to certain beneficiaries.

By categorizing assets, you create a structured overview of your estate, simplifying valuation, management, and, ultimately, the distribution process, ensuring that your wishes are accurately fulfilled.

Tracking & Locating Your Assets

Effective tracking and locating of your assets ensures that they can be easily managed and distributed according to your estate plan. Utilize a comprehensive asset register, which is a detailed document listing all your assets, including their locations, ownership details, and relevant access information. This register should be kept up to date and stored securely with a trusted family member, executor, or attorney informed of its location.

For digital assets, consider using a digital asset management tool or a secure password manager to store login credentials, domain names, and other important digital information. Ensure that your executor or a trusted individual knows how to access this tool without compromising the security of your digital assets.

Physical assets, particularly those in safety deposit boxes or storage units, should be documented with clear instructions on access. Include the location, box or unit number, and the location of keys or access codes.

Regularly reviewing and updating your asset register is important, especially after significant life changes such as acquiring new assets or selling others. This proactive approach ensures that your asset inventory reflects your current holdings, smoothing the estate administration process and preventing valuable assets from being overlooked or lost.

Valuing Your Assets: How Much Are They Really Worth?

You're Worth It: Appraisal & Valuation Basics

Understanding the basics of asset appraisal and valuation is fundamental to effective estate planning. Accurate valuations of your assets ensure that your estate is distributed according to your wishes and that your heirs receive their fair share of your legacy.

An **appraisal** is the process of determining the market value of an asset, which can vary significantly depending on factors such as condition, market demand, and economic circumstances.

Professional appraisals are often necessary to determine the current market value for tangible assets like real estate and personal property (such as vehicles, jewelry, and art). Real estate, in particular, requires an appraisal by a licensed professional who evaluates the property's condition, location, and comparable market sales to establish its value. Personal property may also need valuation by specialists, especially for items like antiques or collectibles for which value is subject to market trends and rarity.

Investments and financial accounts, on the other hand, have values that can be more straightforwardly determined based on current market conditions. However, it's crucial to understand the basis of these valuations and their implications for estate taxes and distribution.

Accurate **valuations** play a significant role in estate planning, impacting estate tax calculations, equitable asset distribution among heirs, and the fulfillment of specific bequests. They also provide a clear financial picture of the estate, aiding in planning potential charitable contributions and managing any estate debts or liabilities. Ultimately, ensuring accurate and up-to-date appraisals of your assets protects the integrity of your estate plan.

Market Value vs. Emotional Value

In estate planning and asset distribution, distinguishing between market value and emotional value can be complicated, but it's important because both play distinct roles in shaping decisions and expectations.

Market value refers to the amount an asset would sell for on the open market, determined by factors like demand, condition, and comparables. It's a quantifiable figure that estate planners[2] and appraisers use to evaluate an estate's worth for tax purposes and equitable distribution among heirs.

---

[2] https://www.forbes.com/sites/forbesfinancecouncil/2019/04/15/why-estate-planners-arent-just-for-the-ultra-rich/

Conversely, **emotional value** is subjective and immeasurable, rooted in personal memories, relationships, and sentiments associated with an asset. A family heirloom, for instance, might hold minimal market value but immense emotional value to certain family members, making it irreplaceable and highly cherished.

The challenge in estate planning arises when these values conflict or when beneficiaries place different levels of importance on the emotional value of the same asset. This discrepancy can lead to disputes or hurt feelings during the distribution process. Recognizing the emotional value of assets and addressing them in your estate plan can help mitigate potential conflicts. For example, specific bequests of sentimental items can ensure that they go to the intended beneficiary, honoring the emotional connections while striving for an equitable distribution based on market value for the rest of the estate.

Incorporating both values into estate planning acknowledges the complex nature of assets, ensuring that both financial equity and emotional legacies are preserved. It also allows for peace among beneficiaries and respect for the decedent's wishes.

Understanding Intangible Asset Valuation

Valuing intangible assets such as intellectual property, digital assets, and business goodwill introduces complexities into estate planning due to their unique characteristics and the absence of a physical market. These assets often hold significant value and potential for future earnings, making their accurate appraisal complex for estate tax implications and equitable distribution among heirs.

- **Intellectual property (IP)** encompasses creations of the mind such as patents, trademarks, copyrights, and trade secrets. Valuing

IP requires considering its market potential, exclusivity period, and current income generation. For patents and copyrights, the remaining term of protection is also critical, as it affects the asset's future value.

- **Digital assets** include domain names, online businesses, and cryptocurrency. Their valuation is influenced by factors like market demand, revenue generation, and technological advancements. Cryptocurrencies, for example, are volatile and require valuation at or near the estate planning date to accurately reflect their current market value.

- **Business goodwill** represents the value beyond the physical assets of a business, encompassing reputation, customer loyalty, and brand identity. Goodwill valuation involves analyzing the business' earnings above what's expected from its tangible assets alone, requiring a thorough understanding of the industry and market trends.

Valuing these intangible assets means that you'll need specialized knowledge, and often the engagement of professionals skilled in appraising suc+h assets. Accurate valuation for ensuring fair market value is reflected in the estate is crucial—it minimizes disputes among beneficiaries and ensures compliance with tax regulations. Given their potential for significant value fluctuation, regular reassessment is recommended to maintain the estate plan's accuracy and relevance.

Deciding Whether You Need a Professional Appraiser

Determining when to use a professional appraiser in estate planning can be necessary, particularly for ensuring the accurate valuation of assets. Professional appraisal services become important in several scenarios, especially when dealing with complex or high-value assets such as real estate, unique collectibles, intellectual property, and business interests. These assets often require specialized knowledge to accurately assess their true market value, as they consider current trends, future potential, and unique characteristics.

There are several benefits of engaging a professional appraiser. First, it provides credibility to the asset valuations in your estate, which is especially important for tax purposes and might be scrutinized by the IRS. Accurate appraisals ensure that you're not overpaying taxes or undervaluing assets for your heirs. Second, a professional valuation can prevent disputes among beneficiaries by offering an impartial assessment of an asset's worth, thus supporting equitable distribution based on objective criteria.

Moreover, professional appraisers bring a level of expertise and market insight that goes beyond surface-level evaluations. They can identify factors that might not be apparent to the untrained eye and therefore affect an asset's value. For instance, the value of a piece of art could depend significantly on its provenance, condition, and the artist's market demand—all factors that a professional appraiser is equipped to analyze.

If your estate includes assets with complex valuation considerations or significant worth, hiring a professional appraiser is a prudent step. It ensures the accuracy and fairness of your estate's valuation and safeguards against potential legal challenges and family infighting.

Essential Tips for Organizing Your Financial Information

This House Is Clean: Streamlining Your Financial Documents

Streamlining your financial documents is vital to maintaining an organized estate plan and ensuring that all necessary information is accessible and up to date. **Below are some practical tips to help you tidy up your financial house:**

1. **Consolidate Documents:** Begin by centralizing all your financial documents including bank statements, investment records, insurance policies, and estate-planning documents like wills and trusts. Grouping similar documents together can simplify navigation and management.

2. **Go Digital:** Convert paper documents to digital files when possible. Use a secure digital storage solution to organize files into clearly labeled folders, and ensure that your executor or a trusted individual knows how to access these digital records. Always remember to back up important documents to prevent loss due to hardware failure.

3. **Create a Document Inventory:** Make a comprehensive list of your financial documents, including their location and any instructions for access (e.g., safe combinations or digital passwords). This inventory should be kept in a secure yet accessible location that's known to your executor or a trusted family member.

4. **Regular Review and Update:** Financial situations can change, so review your documents annually to ensure that they reflect your

current circumstances. Update account information, beneficiary designations, and contact details as needed.

5. **Secure Storage for Originals:** Certain documents, such as original wills, property deeds, and marriage certificates, should be stored in a secure location like a fireproof safe or a safety deposit box. Ensure that your executor knows the location and has access if necessary.

By following these steps, you can create a streamlined and efficient system for managing your financial documents, making it easier for you and your loved ones to navigate your estate when the time comes.

Safe Storage Solutions for Financial Information

Securing your financial details can protect against loss, theft, and unauthorized access. Both physical and digital storage solutions offer ways to safeguard these crucial documents, each with its own set of benefits.

Physical Storage Options:

*   **Safes:** Ideal for storing original documents such as wills, deeds, and insurance policies. Opt for a waterproof and fireproof safe to protect against natural disasters.

*   **Safety Deposit Boxes:** Offered by banks, these provide a highly secure option for storing valuable documents. However, consider their accessibility and that the contents might be sealed upon death unless arrangements are made in advance with the bank and your estate executor.

Digital Storage Solutions:

*   **Encrypted Digital Vaults:** Services that offer encrypted storage for digital copies of important documents provide security and

ease of access from anywhere. Ensure that the service complies with robust security standards to protect your data.

- **Cloud Storage Services:** Popular for their convenience, these allow you to access documents from any device. Use strong passwords, two-factor authentication, and encryption to enhance security.

- **External Hard Drives:** Storing documents on an external hard drive offers an offline option to keep them in a safe place. Consider using encryption software to further secure the data.

Regardless of the storage method chosen, ensuring that your executor or a trusted individual knows the location and how to access these documents when needed is critical. Combining physical and digital storage solutions can provide a comprehensive approach to safeguarding your financial information, balancing accessibility with security.

Password, Please: Managing Digital Access to Financial Accounts

In today's digital age, managing and securely storing passwords for financial accounts is vital. As our financial lives become increasingly online, the importance of strong password management becomes more important every day. It ensures that your accounts remain secure from unauthorized access while also guaranteeing that the people you entrust can access them when necessary, especially in the event of your incapacity or death.

The first step in secure password management is to use complex passwords that are difficult to guess. Utilize a combination of letters, numbers, and special characters, and avoid using the same password across multiple accounts. This reduces the risk of multiple accounts being affected if one password is compromised.

Equally important is the method of storing these passwords. Writing them down and keeping them in a physical location can be risky unless secured in a locked safe or similar secure environment. A more secure and efficient method is to use a digital password manager. These services not only store your passwords securely, encrypted behind a master password, but they can also generate strong passwords for you and autofill them when you log in to sites, reducing the temptation to reuse passwords. However, they're not without fault—there have been highly publicized cases of large password-managing websites being hacked in recent years, so do your due diligence and be as safe as possible.

However, ensuring access to these digital accounts for your executor or designated representative upon your death is a challenge that requires careful planning. Some password managers offer emergency access features or the ability to share certain passwords securely. Alternatively, a comprehensive list of accounts and login information can be included in your estate planning documents, stored securely with instructions on accessing your digital password manager.

Managing and securely storing passwords balances accessibility for you and your trusted representatives and security against unauthorized access. When properly handled, it ensures both the safety of your digital financial assets and their accessibility when needed.

Deciding Who Knows What About Your Finances

Determining who should know or access your financial information can help manage your estate and safeguard your assets. This decision impacts your privacy and security, ensuring that your financial matters can be appropriately handled if you can't manage them yourself or after your passing.

First, consider appointing a trusted individual, such as a spouse, adult child, or close family friend, as well as a legal or financial professional like an attorney or financial advisor. Those selected should be trustworthy and financially literate, and they also need to understand your wishes and estate planning goals.

Protecting Yourself from Bad Actors: A Cautionary Tale from Dane Cook

Consider this: Even your family can surprise you, and not necessarily in a good way. Take comedian Dane Cook's story, for example. Cook trusted his own brother to manage his millions, only to find out he was being robbed blind. It's a harsh reminder that when it comes to money, sometimes the people closest to you can turn out to be the ones you should've watched more closely.

What's the takeaway? Always double-check who you're trusting with your cash. You can hope for the best, but you need to plan for the worst, too. Make sure that there are checks and balances in place. Maybe that means having more than one person keeping an eye on things or setting up regular check-ins on your accounts, just to keep everything honest. This isn't about not trusting your family—it's about protecting what you've worked so hard for.

For daily financial management, you might limit access to someone who helps with bill payments or financial organization. However, comprehensive knowledge of your entire financial portfolio should be reserved for those who'll take on significant roles, such as your executor or power of attorney. To execute your wishes effectively, these people need a thorough understanding of your assets, liabilities, and estate plans.

It's also necessary to consider the circumstances under which access to your financial information is needed. Setting up clear guidelines for when and how your financial details should be disclosed—such as in the event of incapacitation or death—can prevent unauthorized access and ensure a smooth transition of financial management responsibilities.

Lastly, regular discussions and updates with those accessing your financial information are essential. These conversations can clarify your intentions, update any changes in your financial situation, and reaffirm your trust in their abilities to manage your affairs according to your wishes.

Beyond Tangible Assets: Your Digital Assets & Intellectual Property

Recognizing & Managing Digital Assets

Digital assets are a broad range of electronic records and online accounts, including social media profiles, email accounts, digital photos and videos, online banking and investment accounts, domain names, and cryptocurrency. As our lives become increasingly digital, the importance of these assets in estate planning has grown, both for their monetary and sentimental value.

Managing and including digital assets in your estate plan requires several strategies. First, create a comprehensive inventory of your digital assets, detailing login information, passwords, and instructions for each account. This inventory should be kept secure but also accessible to your executor or designated digital executor.

The Digital Dilemma: A Cautionary Tale of Lost Cryptocurrency

In the evolving world of digital currencies, the story of Quadriga CX and its CEO Gerald Cotten serves as a stark reminder of the vulnerabilities inherent to managing digital assets. Cotten's unexpected demise left the exchange in a precarious situation—it was unable to access $145 million in various cryptocurrencies stored in cold wallets, for which only Cotten had the passwords. This incident highlights the importance of having robust plans for digital asset management and succession.

The Importance of Safeguards

Cotten was known for his meticulous security measures, having moved the majority of Quadriga CX's digital coins into cold storage to prevent hacking. However, his precautionary steps also created a single point of failure: His passing effectively locked away millions in customer assets. This underscores the necessity for digital asset holders to implement secure yet accessible management strategies that account for unforeseen circumstances.

Lessons Learned

1. **Multiple Access Points:** Ensure that critical digital assets, especially those in cold storage, can be accessed by more than one trusted individual.

2. **Documented Procedures:** Maintain clear, documented instructions for accessing and managing digital assets that can be executed by your estate's executor or a trusted individual.

3. **Legal and Technical Advice:** Seek both legal and technical guidance when setting up mechanisms for digital asset succession to navigate the complexities of digital estate planning effectively.

Gerald Cotten's story is about the loss of digital wealth but also a cautionary tale that emphasizes the need for careful, comprehensive planning in the digital age.

Second, understand the terms of service agreements for each digital platform, as they dictate what can legally be done with your accounts posthumously. Some platforms have established processes for handling accounts of deceased users, while others may require specific instructions in your estate plan.

It's also important to clearly outline your wishes for each digital asset in your will or trust. Specify whether accounts should be deleted, memorialized, or passed on to heirs. For assets with financial value such as domain names or cryptocurrency, provide detailed instructions on accessing and managing these.

Lastly, consider using a digital estate-planning service or digital vault to store access information securely, ensuring that your digital executor can fulfill their duties without compromising the security of your digital legacy. By proactively including digital assets in your estate plan, you ensure that they're properly managed and distributed according to your wishes.

I Think, Therefore I Am: The Value of Intellectual Property

Intellectual property (IP) represents a crucial yet often overlooked component of many estates. It encompasses creations of the mind such as inventions (patents); literary and artistic works (copyrights); symbols, names, and images used in commerce (trademarks); and trade secrets. IP can hold significant monetary value, potentially generating ongoing revenue streams from royalties, licensing agreements, or outright sale.

Additionally, IP can carry substantial sentimental value, representing an individual's creative legacy.

Identifying IP within an estate first requires a thorough inventory of the creator's output. This may involve cataloging published works, registered and unregistered patents, trademarks associated with personal or business brands, and any proprietary knowledge or processes classified as trade secrets. Given the varying nature of IP rights and the different ways that they're protected legally, consulting with an IP attorney is advisable to ensure that all valuable IP is accurately identified and appropriately valued.

Incorporating IP into estate planning is needed for several reasons. Legally, it ensures that these assets are transferred according to the creator's wishes, whether to heirs, businesses, or charitable organizations. Financially, it allows for the continued management and exploitation of the IP to benefit designated beneficiaries. Moreover, detailing how IP should be handled, maintained, or disposed of can prevent disputes among heirs and preserve the creator's legacy as intended.

Acknowledging and planning for transferring intellectual property rights is a necessary step that can't be overlooked. It not only safeguards the financial interests of your estate but also honors and perpetuates your creative contributions.

Preserving Personal Memories & Keepsakes

From family photos and letters to heirloom jewelry and handmade quilts, personal memories and keepsakes carry immeasurable sentimental value and, in some cases, significant monetary worth. These items are tangible links to our past, connecting generations and preserving the essence of personal and family histories. Their preservation is about safeguarding objects as well as maintaining a legacy and personal identity for future generations.

To ensure that these treasures are preserved, make certain to include them in your estate planning. Documenting the existence and the desired distribution of such items can prevent family disputes and ensure they reach the intended recipients. Professional appraisals can be helpful for items with monetary value, especially for insurance purposes or equitable distribution among heirs.

Physical preservation is also key. Consider the appropriate storage or display conditions to prevent deterioration—acid-free boxes for old photographs, temperature-controlled environments for antique furniture, and safety deposit boxes for valuable jewelry. Digital preservation offers another layer of security, especially for irreplaceable items like family photos or videos, through scanning or digital recording.

Lastly, sharing the stories behind these keepsakes can add to their value, offering context and deepening the emotional connection for the recipient. Whether through written histories, video recordings, or casual storytelling, passing down the significance of these items ensures that they remain cherished and appreciated for their full worth.

Incorporating keepsakes into your estate plan with clear instructions and sharing their stories ensures that these personal treasures continue to be celebrated, preserving your legacy and the rich tapestry of your family's history.

The Secret Life of Data: Privacy in Digital Estate Planning

Estate planning extends beyond tangible assets to encompass a range of digital assets, from social media accounts to online banking information. However, managing these assets raises significant privacy concerns, meaning that you'll need to use careful consideration to protect sensitive information.

First, inventory your digital assets and decide which should be preserved, transferred, or deleted upon your passing. This inventory should include login credentials, but these details must be stored securely to prevent unauthorized access during and after your lifetime. Using a digital estate-planning service or a secure password manager that permits designated individuals access in specific circumstances can safeguard this information.

Legal documents such as wills or trusts should reference digital assets but avoid listing specific passwords or sensitive details directly within these documents, as they may become public during the probate process. Instead, provide instructions on where to find this securely stored information.

Furthermore, appointing a digital executor (an individual tasked with managing your digital legacy) can ensure that your privacy preferences are honored. This role involves distributing or archiving digital assets and handling personal data according to your wishes, which could include deleting emails, closing online accounts, or archiving digital photos.

Protecting the privacy of your digital assets requires a blend of strategic planning, secure information storage, and clear communication with your estate executor and beneficiaries. By taking these steps, you can ensure that your digital legacy is managed respectfully and follows your wishes, safeguarding both your assets and your privacy.

Key Takeaways

- **Comprehensive Inventory:** Thoroughly listing all assets, including digital and intangible ones, is foundational for effective estate management.

- **Importance of Details:** Detailed documentation, including locations and access information, is critical for smooth asset distribution.

- **Asset Classification:** Categorizing assets into clearly defined classes simplifies valuation and management, thereby aiding in the estate planning process.

- **Valuation Nuances:** Understanding the difference between market and emotional value is key to fair asset distribution and tax planning.

- **Digital and Intellectual Property:** Recognizing and valuing digital assets and intellectual property requires special consideration in estate planning.

- **Privacy and Security:** Managing digital access and protecting sensitive information is essential for securely including digital assets in your estate plan.

Chapter 3

Protecting Your Loved Ones Through Estate Planning

"[To leave a legacy] is to plant trees under whose shade you do not expect to sit."
-Nelson Henderson, Author and agriculturist

Trust Funds: Ensuring Your Children's Future

You want to secure a bright and stable future for your children, and trust funds can be the solution, offering financial security with thoughtful planning and care. This chapter examines how trust funds can be a great tool in your estate planning, ensuring that your children's financial needs are met, even in your absence.

The Bank of Mom & Dad: Understanding Trust Funds

Setting up a trust fund is like the ultimate way of saying, "Hey, I've got your back" to your kids, even when you're not around to say it in person. Think of it as the Bank of Mom and Dad but on autopilot. Trust funds aren't just for the ultra-rich—they're a practical tool for any parent looking to secure their child's financial future.

To explain the concept of a trust fund, imagine you're putting money or assets into a special box. You give someone you trust (your trustee) the key and instructions for when and how to open it for your kids. Maybe it's for their college tuition, medical emergencies, or to ensure that they have a safety net for life's ups and downs.

The best part? You get to set the rules. You can decide that the money is for education expenses first and foremost. Or you can set it up so that your kids get a bit of the fund at certain milestones like graduating college, turning a certain age, or even when they land their first real job. It's all focused on making sure that they're taken care of in the ways you think are best.

Trust funds are a way to still provide your love and support, covering everything from school books to emergency room visits, long after you've watched them graduate or walk down the aisle. It's one of those parenting moves that's as smart as it is heartfelt.

Choosing a Trustee for Your Children's Trust

The most important thing to start with is picking the right trustee for your kids' trust. Think of a trustee like the captain of a ship, steering your assets according to the map you've drawn up. This person will make sure that your kids get what they need when they need it according to the wishes you've laid out. Clearly, choosing the right person for this job is extremely important.

First, you want someone responsible and trustworthy, but it's not just about simply picking your most reliable buddy. This person needs to have a good head on their shoulders when it comes to money matters because they'll be calling the shots on investments and distributions. They're the one who'll be ensuring that the trust does what it's supposed to do for your kids.

The role of a trustee isn't just about managing the cash—it's also about understanding your wishes and your kids' needs. Let's say you've set aside money for education. In this case, your trustee will handle the expenses directly related to that like tuition fees, books, and maybe even a study-abroad program. They're also on deck for healthcare and day-to-day living expenses, ensuring that your kids are supported financially until they're ready to take the reins themselves.

Choosing a trustee is a big decision. Some go with family members, thinking that they'll naturally have the kids' best interests at heart. Others opt for a trusted friend, or even a professional like an attorney or a financial advisor, to keep things impartial. Whichever route you choose, make sure that it's someone who gets your family, understands your goals, and can easily navigate the financial world.

Pros and Cons of Trust Funds

Trust funds can be a double-edged sword. On the one hand, they're fantastic tools for securing your loved ones' futures and making sure that they're taken care of long after you're gone. But, like anything else, they come with their own challenges.

Pros:

- **Control and Protection:** Trust funds give you control over how your assets are used. If you'd like to make sure that your kid's college tuition is covered or perhaps ensure that they don't blow their inheritance on a flashy car at 18, a trust can make that happen. Also, it protects those assets from creditors and, in some cases, from making a dent in divorce settlements.

- **Skipping Probate:** Because trust assets aren't part of your estate in the traditional sense, they don't go through probate. This means that your beneficiaries can access them much faster without the legal complications.

Cons:

- **Complexity and Cost:** Setting up a trust isn't like opening a savings account. It's complex and can be expensive due to legal fees. You'll need a knowledgeable attorney who knows what they're doing.

- **Potential Impact on Motivation:** This is where things might get tricky. While you want to provide for your loved ones, there's a distinction between supporting them and inadvertently stifling their drive. If someone knows that they've got a safety net, it might impact their motivation to achieve things independently. It's about finding that balance and ensuring that the trust encourages growth rather than dependency.

Ultimately, trust funds are powerful estate-planning tools but are not one-size-fits-all. They're part of a broader conversation about how we want to support our loved ones and encourage their independence while still providing a solid safety net.

Guardianship Considerations in Estate Planning

Including your wishes for guardianship in your estate plan is important because it's about making sure that you have the right person take care of your children. Let's understand why naming a guardian is so important and what it means both legally and emotionally.

First, if you don't pick someone, the court will. And while they do their best, they don't know your kids like you do. They won't know that Aunt

Jane, despite her wacky lifestyle, shares a special bond with your little ones or that your best friend has values closely aligned with yours. Deciding on a guardian means choosing a future for your kids that you can feel good about, one in which they're loved and raised in a way that you'd approve of.

Legally, it comes down to ensuring that there's no room for uncertainty or lengthy court battles that can stress out your family and eat into your estate. You're basically handing someone the legal authority to make decisions for your kids, from healthcare to education and everything in between.

Emotionally, you're choosing the person to provide a loving, stable home and help your kids to navigate the world without you. It's about making sure that they have someone to celebrate their successes, comfort them through the tough times, and guide them as they grow.

Nominating a guardian is one of the most profound decisions you'll make in your estate plan. It's about peace of mind and knowing that your children's welfare is implicitly in the hands of someone you trust.

Providing for Your Spouse: Survivorship Rights & Marital Property

Till Death Do Us Part: Understanding Survivorship Rights

Next, we need to explore the concept of survivorship rights, which might sound a bit legalistic but is actually incredibly important for couples. Imagine you and your spouse own a house together—you want to make sure that if something happens to one of you, the other doesn't have to fight tooth and nail to keep the roof over their head. That's where survivorship rights come into play.

Survivorship rights help with many things—especially real estate—and basically means that you're saying, "When I'm gone, this goes straight to my partner." No detours and no probate court drama—just a straight pass from you to them. There are two ways in which couples can own things to ensure that this happens: joint tenancy and tenancy by the entirety.

Joint tenancy is like team ownership; you both own the whole thing together. If one team member bows out, the other automatically becomes the sole owner of the entire asset. It's a way to ensure that your significant other doesn't have to wrangle with legal processes just to stay in their own home.

Tenancy by the entirety is similar but exclusively for married couples. It adds an extra layer of protection, shielding your assets from individual debts. If one spouse has financial troubles, this setup keeps the shared asset out of reach from creditors.

Using these tools means you're thinking ahead and ensuring that your spouse is cared for without the hassle of probate. It's like saying, "Till death do us part, but I've got your back even after that."

Ensuring That Your Spouse is Financially Secure

When it comes to estate planning, making sure that your spouse is taken care of financially after you're gone is the best inheritance you can give them. It's about knowing that your spouse can keep living their life without a financial cloud hanging over them, and a great way to provide this is through life insurance.

Life insurance isn't just a policy but rather a promise. A promise that, come what may, your partner won't have to worry about money. It can be a game changer, whether it's paying off the mortgage or covering daily living expenses. Also, it skips the probate process and goes directly to your spouse when they need it most.

Then there's the two retirement account options. If you've been stashing away money in an IRA or a 401(k), you have a golden opportunity to support your spouse's future. By naming them as the beneficiary, you ensure that they have access to these funds directly, again bypassing the probate process. And the best part is that some accounts let your spouse roll the funds into their own IRA, keeping the tax-deferred benefits ongoing.

Incorporating these strategies into your estate plan is essentially setting up a safety net for your spouse, ensuring that they're taken care of and can maintain the lifestyle you've built together. After all, estate planning is as much about love as it is legacies.

Navigating Marital Property Laws

Discussing marital property laws might not be your typical conversation, but it's a conversation worth having when it comes to estate planning. Where you live plays a big role in how your assets are divided when you or your spouse pass away. It's all about understanding the lay of the land, whether you're in a community property state or not.

In **community property** states, the law regards most of what you and your spouse acquired during your marriage as jointly owned. Think of it like a big communal pot—both of you have equal dibs on everything in it, from your house to your savings account regardless of whose name is on the paycheck. When it comes to estate planning, knowing that half of the communal pot automatically goes to your spouse is the first step.

Then there's the rest of the country, where **separate property** rules apply. Here, it's more about who owns what. If you bought something before you married or received it as a gift or inheritance in your name, it's likely considered your separate property. This distinction is important for estate planning because it affects how you can pass on your assets.

Understanding these nuances can help you with the estate planning process and ensure that your assets end up where you want them to be. Whether it's making sure your spouse is taken care of or passing on heirlooms to your kids, knowing the rules in your state is paramount.

I Do (Again): Estate Planning for Second Marriages

Tying the knot again brings a lot of joy and a bit of complexity to the table, especially when it comes to estate planning for blended families. You need to make sure that the end result is harmonious and reflects everyone involved.

One of the main challenges is ensuring that your assets are distributed in a way that takes care of everyone, from your new spouse to your kids from a previous marriage and any new family members you've gained along the way. It's a delicate balancing act trying to make sure that everyone feels valued and protected.

Prenuptial agreements are a solid idea to get started with. They allow you to specify exactly how you want your assets handled if things don't go as planned, either through separation or if you pass away. While not exactly enjoyable to discuss, it helps to ensure that everyone's on the same page and that your wishes are clear.

Trusts are another essential tool. They give you the flexibility to provide for your new spouse while also setting aside assets for your children from previous marriages.

Navigating estate planning in second marriages is all about clear communication, careful planning, and a bit of legal savvy. With the right approach, you can ensure that your blended family is supported and your legacy is preserved just as you envision.

Aging: Long-Term Care & Elder Law

Planning for Yourself & Your Living Parents

Estate planning isn't just about looking after your future but also about caring for your parents while they're still here. Let's examine why your estate strategy should include plans for long-term care and healthcare directives.

First, you need to consider long-term care costs. Nobody likes to think about the possibility of their parents (or even themselves) needing assistance with daily living as they age, but it's a reality that many of us will face. Factoring in the potential cost of home care, assisted living, or nursing home care into your estate plan can prevent any financial surprises. Finding quality care that's accessible without draining the family's resources or burdening your children can be challenging.

There's also the matter of healthcare directives and powers of attorney. These aren't just formal documents—they're also your voice when you or your parents can't speak for yourselves. A healthcare directive lays out the types of medical care that you or your parents would want, aligning with your personal beliefs and preferences. On the other hand, a power of attorney appoints someone you trust to make decisions on your behalf. It's about maintaining control over your healthcare and ensuring that decisions are made by someone who understands your wishes.

Incorporating these elements into your estate plan is a gesture of love and respect for your parent's dignity and autonomy. It ensures that as they enter their golden years, they do so with the peace of mind that their care and preferences are honored.

Determining Executor & Healthcare Directives

Next on your list should be picking the right executor for your estate and securing any healthcare directives. Think of it as setting up the ultimate dream team for when you're not around to take care of things.

First, your executor will step into your shoes and make sure that all your estate-planning wishes are carried out to the letter. They'll pay off your debts, distribute your assets, and even deal with any final tax returns. Choosing someone who's organized and trustworthy and who can handle a bit of pressure is key.

The next thing to consider is healthcare directives. While your executor handles your property and assets after you're gone, your healthcare directive is all about making your medical wishes known while you're still here but maybe can't speak for yourself. It's about decisions like whether you want life support, what kind of end-of-life care you prefer, and who can make medical decisions on your behalf if you're unable to.

While the executor and healthcare directive serve different roles, they're both important in respecting your wishes. One is for your assets and the other is for your health. Getting these in place is a way of looking out for your loved ones by making tough times a little easier for them to navigate.

Living Wills and Other Tough Conversations

Navigating the topic of living wills and end-of-life care preferences with your family is all about balance. Living wills, which are crucial documents that spell out your wishes for medical treatment if you cannot communicate, play an enormous role. They're your voice during times when you can't speak for yourself, ensuring that your healthcare preferences are known and respected.

However, having a living will is only half the battle. The other half is sitting down with your loved ones and having those tough, heart-to-heart conversations about what you want at the end of your journey. While not exactly light chat, it's one of the most profound gifts you can give your family. It's about removing the guesswork and the "what-ifs" that can hover over a family during challenging times.

Initiating these discussions takes courage. It requires opening up, sharing your values and desires, and, most importantly, listening. It's a two-way street. By expressing your wishes clearly, you're not just planning for the unforeseeable—you're also providing your family with clarity and stability. When they know what you want, it eases the burden of decision making and allows them to focus on what's truly important, which is cherishing the time you spend together.

It's Inevitable: Elder Law Considerations

Elder law is like a compass for navigating the later years of life, pointing the way through complex legal terrain that includes estate planning, healthcare, and protection against abuse. It's a specialized field that focuses on the unique needs of older adults, ensuring that they're not just preparing for the future but are also shielded from the vulnerabilities that can come with aging.

You're looking at the broader picture when weaving elder law into your estate planning. It comes down to ensuring a quality of life for your golden years and protecting yourself from potential risks. Elder law addresses aspects like long-term care planning, medical directives, and even guardianship, laying a foundation for your wishes and well-being to be respected as you age.

A large component of elder law is safeguarding against abuse and financial exploitation. Sadly, the elderly are often targets for these threats, sometimes from strangers and, heartbreakingly, even from within their own families. Elder law provides some safety, with legal tools and resources designed to protect assets and personal dignity. This includes everything from setting up trusts to keep finances secure to appointing a trusted advocate who can step in if there's ever a hint of mistreatment.

Crucial Functions of Trustees, Custodians & Surety Bonds

Think of these roles and tools as the guardians of your assets, each playing a part in making sure everything you've worked for is managed and passed on just the way you want.

Trustees are like the captains of your ship—they steer your estate according to the map you've drawn up in your trust documents. Whether it's distributing assets to beneficiaries, managing investments, or making sure that all taxes and bills are paid, trustees are on the front line ensuring that your wishes are carried out exactly as you've specified.

Custodians, on the other hand, are the keepers of your assets. They're responsible for holding and safeguarding everything from stocks and bonds to the deeds of your properties. While they might not make the big decisions like trustees do, their role in keeping your assets secure is still vital.

Then there's the surety bond, a kind of insurance policy for your estate. It's there to protect the estate against the possibility of a trustee or executor not fulfilling their duties or, worse, acting dishonestly. If something goes wrong, the surety bond covers any losses, offering an extra layer of security to ensure that your estate is managed faithfully.

Trustees, custodians, and surety bonds form a robust defense, safeguarding your estate and ensuring that your assets are well-protected and faithfully managed.

Generational Wealth Transfer: Leaving a Legacy for Future Generations

The Importance of Generational Wealth Transfer

Generational wealth[3] transfer is a gift that keeps on giving to your family. It's about ensuring that the fruits of your labor benefit not just your children but also potentially their kids and beyond. But how do

---

[3] https://www.investopedia.com/generational-wealth-definition-5189580

you pass on this legacy without a hefty chunk becoming lost to taxes or otherwise?

One key strategy is the use of trusts. Trusts can allow you to control how and when your assets are distributed, which can significantly reduce the tax hit. For example, a properly structured trust can bypass probate, reduce estate taxes, and ensure that your wealth reaches your descendants according to your wishes while keeping Uncle Sam's hands off as much as possible.

Another tool is gifting. You can start passing on your wealth during your lifetime by taking advantage of annual gift tax exclusions and educational or medical expense exemptions. This reduces the size of your taxable estate and allows you to see the benefits of your generosity play out in real time.

The impact of successfully transferring wealth across generations is profound. It can provide a financial head start for your descendants and allow for educational opportunities, entrepreneurial endeavors, or simply a safety net.

Essentially, generational wealth transfer, done thoughtfully, can be one of the most impactful ways you contribute to your family's legacy, shaping their futures in profound and lasting ways.

The Vanderbilts' Lost Fortune

Once America's wealthiest family, the Vanderbilts amassed a fortune in the late 19th century, a sum that's equivalent to billions today. Cornelius Vanderbilt, the patriarch, built his wealth from railroads and shipping. Despite its immense wealth, the Vanderbilt family saw its fortune dwindle over generations due to extravagant spending and lack of financial education among heirs. By the mid-20th century, the once vast Vanderbilt fortune had largely evaporated.

This story underscores the critical importance of transferring wealth and educating heirs on managing and preserving it. It illustrates how even the greatest fortunes can be lost without proper planning and financial stewardship, emphasizing the need for estate planning, including generational wealth education.

Your Family Business: Estate Planning Essentials

Things can get tricky when weaving your family business into your estate plan. Your family business is a legacy, potentially providing for future generations. But the transfer can easily be convoluted without a solid plan, putting the business and your family's financial future at risk.

First, consider your business' structure and how it aligns with your estate-planning[4] goals. Whether it's a partnership, corporation, or sole proprietorship, each has implications for how the business can be transferred and how it'll be taxed. It's about finding the right fit that ensures continuity while minimizing tax implications.

Succession planning is key, and so you need to decide who'll take the reins and prepare them for the responsibility. This might involve training within the business, formal education, or bringing in outside managers. The goal is to ensure that the business survives the transition and continues to thrive.

---

[4] https://www.legalzoom.com/articles/what-you-need-to-know-about-estate-planning

Also, consider how to handle family members who aren't involved in the business. Balance fairness with the business' needs, using tools like life insurance to provide for them without draining the business' resources.

Incorporating your family business into your estate plan with care and foresight ensures that your legacy endures, supports your family, and serves your community for generations. It's about passing on wealth, values, vision, and the spirit of entrepreneurship.

The Case of Aretha Franklin

Despite her substantial estate, "Queen of Soul" Aretha Franklin passed away in 2018 without a will. This grand oversight led to a complicated legal battle among her heirs. Regardless of Franklin's significant assets, the lack of clear estate planning directives put her family in a difficult position, sparking disputes over her estate that could've been avoided with proper planning.

Franklin's case highlights the importance of having a will or trust in place, especially for those with considerable assets. It's a cautionary tale about the potential for family conflict and legal complications when estate planning is neglected, emphasizing the need to secure a spouse's and family's financial future through thoughtful estate planning.

Charitable Giving as a Part of Your Legacy

Incorporating philanthropy into your estate plan can create an impact far beyond your expectations. It's a way to ensure that your legacy extends beyond your family, touching communities and causes close to your heart.

Utilizing your estate plan for charitable giving reflects your values and the causes you believe in. Whether it's a scholarship fund at your alma mater, a bequest to a beloved charity, or support for a local animal shelter, these gifts ensure that your philanthropic goals continue long after you're gone. Also, integrating charitable giving into your estate plan can offer tangible benefits, including tax advantages that can increase the value of your estate for both your heirs and the organizations you choose to support.

For the organizations you care about, receiving support through legacy giving can be transformative. It provides them with the resources to plan for the future, expand their services, and make a more significant impact. And for you, the donor, it's an opportunity to be remembered as someone who made a difference and used their success to fuel positive change.

Preparing Heirs for Wealth Transfer

This is a huge step in making sure that your legacy continues. Educating heirs about the financial management and responsibilities that come with wealth is crucial, setting them up not just for success but also for meaningful stewardship of their inheritance.

As previously noted, education is key. This doesn't mean just formal education but also real, practical guidance on managing finances, understanding investments, and navigating the complexities of wealth. Create opportunities for heirs to learn the value of money, the importance of budgeting, and the power of compound interest. Workshops, family meetings, and even mentorship programs can be valuable in teaching these skills.

But it's not all about the numbers—instilling a sense of responsibility and purpose is equally important. Encouraging philanthropy and involvement in charitable causes helps heirs see their wealth as a tool for good, fostering a sense of duty to give back and make a difference. Sharing stories of family philanthropy, involving heirs in charitable decisions, and even setting up charitable trusts or foundations can inspire a legacy of giving.

Preparing heirs for wealth transfer comes down to passing on values, encouraging responsible stewardship, and ensuring that future generations use their inheritance to lead fulfilling lives and contribute to their communities. This preparation ensures that the wealth transfer catalyzes positive impact, echoing the family's legacy through generations.

The Walton Family Legacy

Unlike the Vanderbilts, the Walton family, heirs to the Walmart empire, is often cited as a model for successful generational wealth transfer. Founder Sam Walton imparted not only his wealth but also his business acumen and frugal values to his children. Today, the Walton family continues to grow its fortune (around $260 billion as of 2023), largely due to the emphasis on financial education and responsible wealth management from an early age.

The Waltons' approach showcases the positive impact of preparing heirs for wealth transfer through education, as well as involvement in the family's business and philanthropic efforts. Their story serves as a powerful example of how fostering financial literacy and a sense of stewardship can preserve and enhance a family's legacy through generations.

Key Takeaways

1. **Choosing a Trustee:** The selection of a trustee is crucial. This individual should be trustworthy and financially savvy, as well as aligned with your family's values and the specific needs of your beneficiaries. Their role in managing and distributing trust assets is central to the trust's success.

2. **Navigating Survivorship Rights:** For married couples, understanding survivorship rights and how assets are titled can ensure the smooth transfer of wealth to the surviving spouse, bypassing the probate process and maintaining the family's financial security.

3. **Estate Planning for Second Marriages:** Blended families face unique challenges in estate planning. Tools like prenuptial agreements and trusts are vital for protecting assets for children from previous marriages, while also providing for the current spouse.

4. **Long-Term Care and Elder Law:** Including plans for long-term care and elder law considerations in your estate plan protects your future and that of your aging parents, ensuring that everyone's care preferences and financial needs are addressed.

5. **Generational Wealth Transfer:** Effective estate planning facilitates the transfer of wealth across generations, minimizing tax burdens and reinforcing the family's legacy through shared values and goals.

6. **Educating Heirs:** Preparing heirs for wealth transfer involves more than just handing over assets. It's also about educating them on financial management, instilling a sense of stewardship, and encouraging philanthropy to ensure the responsible continuation of the family's legacy.

Chapter 4

DIY Estate Planning & Choosing the Right Lawyer

"The bitterness of poor quality remains long after the sweetness of low price is forgotten."
- Benjamin Franklin, American Founding Father and inventor

DIY Estate Planning: When Is It Feasible?

Getting into DIY estate planning might be intimidating at first, but it's absolutely achievable with the right tools and information at your disposal. In this chapter, we'll address when tackling estate planning on your own makes sense while also highlighting some online tools that can help guide you through the process.

Pros & Cons of DIY Estate Planning

An advantage of DIY estate planning is that it can save you some money, and there's also a certain pride in doing things yourself. With plenty of online guides and forms at your fingertips, it can be tempting to bypass the lawyer's fees and have your will or basic estate plan sorted inexpensively.

However, estate law is tricky and full of little nuances that can make things muddled. Just as every state has its own quirks about what makes a will valid, missing a single step or not wording something correctly can land you in trouble. Suddenly, the document you spent hours on doesn't hold water legally, and fixing that mess isn't not cheap. Trying to patch up or defend a DIY plan gone wrong can end up costing far more than if you'd simply gone to a professional from the start.

So while the DIY route is definitely lighter on your finances at first glance, it's also somewhat of a gamble. It comes down to how comfortable you feel navigating legal jargon and ticking all the right boxes on your own. If there's any doubt, perhaps saving money upfront isn't worth the potential headache later. After all, peace of mind has its own value—especially when it comes to making sure that your estate is in good hands.

Tech to the Rescue: Online Tools to Simplify Estate Planning

Estate planning has essentially hitched a ride on the coattails of technology, making the process convenient, efficient, and more accessible than ever. Gone are the days when drafting a will meant a somber sit-down in your lawyer's office. Now, plenty of online platforms are at your service, turning what used to be an intimidating task into something you can take care of from your living room couch with a coffee in your hand.

These digital additions range from simple will-writing tools to more comprehensive estate planning software that walk you through trusts, powers of attorney, and health care directives. They're designed with the user in mind, making legal jargon easier to digest and ensuring that you don't miss out on any crucial steps. For many, it's a game changer, opening up access to estate planning that was previously too costly or intimidating.

But the problem is that not all online tools are created equal. The law isn't static, which means that the estate planning tool that was useful a year ago might now be out of date. Before you put your trust (and your estate) into the hands of a digital platform, check that it's keeping pace with the latest in state laws. After all, an outdated will is useless.

So while tech has indeed come to the rescue in making estate planning more accessible, the onus is still on you to ensure that the tools you use are sharp and up-to-date. The bottom line is that when it comes to safeguarding your legacy, cutting corners could cut deep.

The following are a few estate-planning tools that may be able to help:

1. **Quicken WillMaker & Trust:** Known for its ease of use, Quicken WillMaker & Trust offers a solution for creating a customized estate plan including wills, trusts, health care directives, and financial powers of attorney.

2. **LegalZoom:** This platform provides legal services online, including estate planning documents like wills and trusts. LegalZoom also offers access to legal advice from licensed attorneys.

3. **Rocket Lawyer:** This useful tool offers an online estate-planning service with the option to create legal documents and consult with attorneys.

4. **Trust & Will:** Specializing in estate planning, Trust & Will aims to make the process of creating wills and trusts as straightforward as possible, with options to update documents as life changes.

Risky Business: Common Pitfalls in DIY Estate Planning

DIY estate planning can feel like you're taking control of your future without waiting on anyone else, but you need to tread carefully. This realm is filled with confusing pitfalls that can complicate things if you're not vigilant. Estate planning missteps, like not properly executing documents, can leave your plans unstable and your loved ones in a bind.

One common hiccup is the failure to follow through with all the formalities required for legal documents. Each state has its own set of rules about what makes a will or trust valid. Skip a step, like missing witnesses or a notary for your will, and your plans won't carry any legal weight whatsoever.

In addition, there's the complexity of your estate to consider. If your situation involves more than the basics, like businesses, out-of-state properties, or a blended family, going it alone can be a real challenge. What seems like a money-saver upfront could end up costing your heirs time and money in probate court.

This isn't to say that you shouldn't explore DIY options, especially for simpler estates. However, you need to know when to call in the professionals. A bit of expert advice can prevent significant headaches down the road.

Philip Seymour Hoffman's Estate Planning Misstep

Acclaimed actor Philip Seymour Hoffman passed away in 2014, leaving behind an estate valued at approximately $35 million. Despite his substantial assets, Hoffman had a notably simple will, one that hadn't been updated for years. His will left the bulk of his estate to his longtime partner Mimi O'Donnell, with whom he had three children. However, because Hoffman and O'Donnell weren't married, his estate faced significant estate taxes, with estimates suggesting that more than $12 million went to tax payments.

This story underscores the importance of not only having an estate plan but also ensuring that it's thoroughly considered and up-to-date. Hoffman's situation highlights how failing to account for the legal intricacies of estate and tax planning can result in a significant portion of one's estate going to taxes rather than to intended beneficiaries.

The Good, the Bad & the Ugly: Stories of DIY Estate Planning

The Good: The Case of the Meticulous Planner

Susan, a retired teacher, decided to tackle her estate plan head-on. Armed with comprehensive guides and utilizing a reputable online legal platform, she created her will, a durable power of attorney, and an advanced healthcare directive. She researched her state's laws to ensure compliance and had her documents reviewed by a lawyer through a low-cost legal clinic. Susan's thoroughness paid off. When she passed away, her estate was settled smoothly without any disputes, proving that with diligence and the right resources, DIY estate planning can work well.

The Bad: Overlooking Important Details

Tom, an avid DIY enthusiast, used a free online template to draft his will. Believing that his situation was straightforward, he didn't seek legal advice. Unfortunately, however, Tom failed to properly execute the document according to his state's requirements, rendering the will invalid. His assets went through intestate succession, distributed in a way that contradicted his wishes and caused unnecessary stress for his family.

The Ugly: The Case of the Lost Assets

Emily created her estate plan using a DIY service, but she didn't update her beneficiary designations on her retirement accounts and insurance policies. When she passed, those assets were distributed to her ex-husband, instead of her children as she intended in her will. This oversight led to a lengthy legal battle, draining the estate's resources and causing rifts within the family.

These stories emphasize the mixed bag of outcomes with DIY estate planning. While it's possible to successfully navigate the process, the risks of overlooking legal nuances or failing to update critical documents can have lasting consequences on your estate and your loved ones.

Ann Aldrich's Case – The Trouble with Not Updating

A well-known case in Florida law, Ann used a DIY kit to draft her will, clearly outlining how her assets should be distributed among her family members. She thought that everything was in order after listing her assets and to whom they should go. However, Ann later acquired new assets but didn't update her will to include them or specify a residual clause for any future assets. After her passing, a dispute arose among her heirs regarding the distribution of these new assets, leading to a legal battle that reached the Florida Supreme Court. The court ultimately ruled that the assets acquired after the will was written could not be distributed according to the will's existing terms, leading to a default distribution under state law, which was not what Ann had intended.

Legal Fees: What Can You Expect to Pay?

Understanding Legal Fee Structures

Estate planning often involves navigating the maze of legal fee structures, each with its own set of implications for your budget. The basics of flat fees, hourly rates, and contingency fees, though less common in estate planning, can help you make informed decisions on engaging legal services.

Flat fees are increasingly popular for estate planning, offering a clear, upfront cost for specific services such as drafting a will or setting up a basic trust. This model is attractive for its predictability, allowing you to budget precisely without worrying about the ticking clock of billable hours. It would be best to understand exactly what services are included in this flat rate to avoid unexpected charges for additional work.

Hourly rates are traditional in the legal world, in which you pay for the time your attorney spends on your case. This can vary widely depending on the lawyer's experience and location. While hourly billing offers flexibility to adjust the scope of work as needed, it can also introduce uncertainty into your budgeting. Keeping open lines of communication and regularly checking in on billable hours can help manage costs effectively.

Contingency fees, common in personal injury cases, are based on the lawyer receiving a percentage of the settlement or judgment. Given the nature of the work, they're rare in estate planning, but understanding this option is part of a broader legal fee literacy.

Average Costs for Estate Planning Services

In estate planning, figuring out how much you'll need to budget for can be tricky. Costs[5] can vary widely based on what you're looking to accomplish and who's helping you get there. To give you a general idea, let's break down the typical pricing for some of the most common estate planning services.

For starters, drafting a simple, straightforward will might set you back anywhere from $300 to $1,200 if you're working with an attorney. This price tag reflects the professional advice and peace of mind that come with knowing that your will is solid and legally binding.

If you're considering setting up a trust, whether to avoid probate or manage your estate's privacy, costs start to increase. Setting up a basic trust can cost anywhere from $1,500 to $5,000 or more, with the complexity of your estate being a primary price driver. Trusts require more legal legwork than wills, hence the higher cost.

For those needing a comprehensive estate plan that includes a will, one or more trusts, powers of attorney, and healthcare directives, you could be looking at fees ranging from $2,000 to $6,000 and up. The more components you add, the higher the fee—especially if your situation involves unique assets, tax planning, or specific instructions for care and guardianship.

Several factors influence these costs, including your location (lawyers in big cities usually charge more), the attorney's experience level, and the complexity of your estate. While it's tempting to go with the cheapest option, investing in quality legal advice can save you and your heirs time, money, and stress in the long run.

---

[5] https://www.findlaw.com/estate/planning-an-estate/what-does-an-average-estate-plan-cost-detailed-price-analysis.html

There are a few additional legal expenses to be aware of:

- **Taxes:** Be aware of potential estate, inheritance, and gift taxes which can vary by location and estate size.

- **Court Fees:** Probate can incur fees from a few hundred to several thousand dollars, influenced by estate value and process complexity.

- **Appraisal Costs:** Valuing assets like property or art is costly but essential, and is necessary for accurate estate and tax calculations.

- **Comprehensive Budgeting:** Discuss all possible costs, not just drafting fees, with your attorney for a realistic estate-planning budget.

Getting the Most Value for Your Legal Fees

Navigating legal costs for estate planning can ensure that you're getting the most value, so let's delve into a few tips on how to go about this.

First, efficiency is your best friend during legal consultations. Time is money, especially when attorneys charge by the hour. Before meeting with your lawyer, compile all relevant documents—your current will, trust, property deeds, account statements, and any previous estate planning documents. Having these at hand saves time and, by extension, money.

Preparation goes a long way, so draft a list of specific questions or concerns you have about your estate plan. This ensures that you cover all your bases during the consultation and helps your attorney provide focused, relevant advice without the need to backtrack or cover ground in future (potentially billable) conversations.

Clear communication is another thing that's advisable. Be upfront about your budget and what you hope to achieve with your estate plan. An effective lawyer will work with you to prioritize actions based on your financial constraints and estate planning goals.

Lastly, organization can significantly impact your bottom line. Keeping well-organized records, documents, and correspondence can reduce the time your attorney needs to get up to speed, allowing them to concentrate on providing legal advice rather than administrative tasks.

Negotiating with Lawyers: How to Get the Best Deal

Effective Strategies for Negotiating Legal Fees

Haggling[6] over legal fees is a daunting prospect, but the right approach can lead to a lower invoice for your estate planning. Think of it less like a confrontation and more like finding common ground. **Below are some strategies to consider:**

1. First, arm yourself with **knowledge**. Research typical costs for estate planning services in your area so that you have a baseline for negotiations. This puts you in a stronger position to discuss fees because you'll know what's fair and reasonable for the scope of work you need.

2. Next, don't hesitate to ask for a **breakdown of the proposed fees**. Understanding exactly what services you're being charged for and why can open the door to discussions about where there might be

---

[6] https://www.legalmatch.com/law-library/article/negotiating-your-lawyers-hourly-fee.html

wiggle room. Maybe there are services you don't need, or perhaps simpler, more cost-effective ways to achieve your goals.

3. Another effective strategy is to inquire about **alternative billing arrangements**. Instead of the traditional hourly rate, your attorney might be willing to work for a flat fee, especially for more straightforward tasks.

4. Lastly, consider the value of building a **long-term relationship**. Attorneys are more likely to negotiate fees with clients who anticipate needing legal services over time. If you see your estate planning as an ongoing process because life changes and your estate plan should evolve too, mention this.

You can also look to offer value beyond just money, which can make the negotiation easier. Sometimes, establishing a mutually beneficial relationship with your lawyer might involve non-monetary exchanges. **Here's how you can offer value to your lawyer beyond just money, potentially leading to more favorable terms:**

- **Barter Services:** In some instances, you might have a skill or service that's valuable to your lawyer or their firm. Whether it's marketing expertise, web design services, or consulting in a specific industry, proposing a barter arrangement can be a win-win.

- **Referrals:** Lawyers, much like other professionals, thrive on referrals. If you're pleased with the services provided, offering to refer friends, family, or business associates can be incredibly valuable.

- **Testimonials and Reviews:** Positive online reviews and testimonials can impact a lawyer's reputation and ability to attract new clients. Offering to write a detailed review or testimonial about your positive experience can be a way of showing appreciation for their work.

Understanding Your Lawyer's Perspective

This can significantly enhance the client-attorney relationship and help you navigate the cost of estate planning more effectively, especially regarding how your lawyer determines their fees. Lawyers typically consider several factors when setting their fees.

The complexity of your case plays a significant role in determining what you'll be charged. Simple estate plans involving just a will or basic trust might be priced at a flat rate, reflecting the relatively straightforward nature of the work. However, as the complexity increases—perhaps involving multiple trusts, tax planning strategies, or assets in various states—the time and expertise required escalate, often leading to higher fees or hourly billing.

Client preparedness is another factor. Attorneys appreciate clients who come organized, with clear objectives and all necessary documents in hand.

Lawyers also consider the value they provide, balancing the need to be competitively priced with their expertise and personalized service. Understanding these dynamics can help you appreciate the rationale behind legal fees and encourage a more open, productive conversation about managing them effectively for your estate planning needs.

Specialization: Deciding On an Estate Planning Lawyer

Specialists vs. Generalists: The Case for Choosing an Estate Planning Attorney

When safeguarding your legacy and ensuring that your final wishes are respected, choosing between a generalist lawyer and an estate-planning specialist can make all the difference. While both are skilled, the estate planning attorney's expertise may be what you need. The complexities of laws, taxes, and trusts demand specialized knowledge.

Estate planning specialists devote their practice to understanding the nuances of estate law and staying updated on the latest legislative changes that could impact your estate plan. This allows them to navigate complex scenarios, ensuring that your estate plan is effective and legally sound. For instance, they can offer advanced strategies for tax reduction, asset protection, and the seamless transfer of wealth to the next generation.

Specialists might also find opportunities or foresee challenges that might not even cross a generalist's mind. They'll help avoid probate, minimize estate taxes, and protect your beneficiaries, addressing concerns before they become problems.

The ABCs of Estate Planning Law: What a Specialist Brings to the Table

Estate planning law is complicated, with intricate legal statutes, tax codes, and probate procedures, and so navigating it requires someone who knows every twist and turn. This is where an estate planning specialist helps with their deep understanding of this complex legal terrain.

A specialist in estate planning law is deeply familiar with the details that can make or break an estate plan. For example, they understand how different types of trusts can achieve specific goals like avoiding probate, protecting assets from creditors, or providing for a special needs relative. They also know the latest tax laws, ensuring that strategies are optimized to minimize tax for your estate and beneficiaries.

The advantage of this expertise is clear: it provides a more effective, efficient, and tailored estate plan.

The Ripple Effect: How the Right Lawyer Can Save You Time, Money & Stress

Choosing the lawyer that's right for you can create a positive ripple effect across your entire estate plan, influencing not just the immediate handling of your assets but also the long-term well-being of your beneficiaries. A specialist can bring efficiency and savings to the table.

Consider the case of a family business owner who, with the guidance of a specialized attorney, establishes a trust that ensures smooth succession. They can leverage tax advantages, saving the family significant amounts in estate taxes. Or the story of parents with a special needs child, for whom a specialist drafts a comprehensive plan that includes a special needs trust, securing the child's financial future without jeopardizing any eligibility for government benefits.

By aligning the estate plan with current laws and the unique needs of the estate, a specialist can significantly reduce the time and money spent settling one's affairs after passing.

You'll also have more peace of mind knowing that your estate plan is crafted to withstand legal scrutiny and effectively manage your legacy. Being certain that everything is in order reduces stress for you and your heirs and demonstrates the long-term benefits of working with a specialized attorney.

The Interview Process: Questions to Ask Potential Lawyers

Kickstarting the Conversation

The first step to hiring a potential estate-planning attorney is to set up an interview with them. The good news is that everything else can fall into place more smoothly once you've started. **Here's how to initiate the conversation and lay the groundwork for a productive consultation:**

- **Research and Prepare:** Before reaching out, do your homework. Look into the attorney's background, specialties, and reviews from previous clients. Prepare a brief summary of your estate, including assets, family structure, and any specific concerns you may have.

- **First Contact:** Whether by email, phone, or an online form, your initial contact should be concise but informative. Briefly outline your estate planning needs and why you believe that they might be the right fit for you. Ask for an initial consultation (many attorneys offer these free of charge).

- **Clarify Your Goals:** Be clear about what you hope to achieve through estate planning. Whether it's protecting assets for your heirs, ensuring that minor children are cared for, or something else entirely, understanding your priorities will help the attorney during the consultation.

- **Ask About the Process:** Inquire about how they typically work with clients. Understanding the process can help set expectations and make the consultation more efficient.

Essential Questions to Ask a Prospective Lawyer

Now that you've set up the meeting, you need to prepare some questions. The right questions can illuminate your potential lawyer's experience and approach, as well as how closely they align with your needs. This conversation is like a first date, in which you're gauging compatibility and expertise. **The following are some essential questions to ask:**

1. **What is your experience in estate planning?** This question helps you understand their depth of knowledge and specialization in estate planning. Experience with similar estates to yours can be a significant advantage.

2. **How do you customize estate plans to fit individual client needs?** This reveals their approach to tailoring plans based on unique client situations, highlighting their flexibility and creativity in planning.

3. **Can you explain your process for developing an estate plan?** Understanding their process from start to finish helps set expectations for how your case will be handled, the timeline, and the steps involved.

4. **How do you handle changes in laws or personal circumstances?** This question assesses their proactive approach to keeping your estate plan current and adaptable to both legal changes and shifts in your personal life.

5. **What are your communication policies?** Knowing how and when to expect updates or responses can help the working relationship.

6. **Can you provide an estimate of all costs involved?** This question helps avoid any surprises and ensures transparency about fees, including potential additional costs.

Understanding a Lawyer's Approach & Philosophy

Not every lawyer will be the same, so you need to understand their estate planning philosophy and approach to client relationships. This alignment can help build a harmonious working relationship and ensures that your estate plan reflects your values and goals. **Below are a few tips on how to evaluate and match a lawyer's approach with your expectations:**

- **Understanding Their Philosophy:** Start by asking direct questions about their views on estate planning. Are they more conservative, favoring traditional strategies, or do they employ innovative solutions to meet modern challenges? Their philosophy should resonate with your vision for your estate.

- **Client Relationship Approach:** The lawyer's stance on client relationships can significantly influence your experience. Do they view clients as partners in the planning process, or is their approach more directive? A collaborative relationship often results in a more personalized and satisfying estate plan.

- **Communication Style:** Compatibility in communication style is key. Whether you prefer detailed explanations or high-level summaries, ensure that their communication style aligns with how you best understand and process information.

- **Evaluating Compatibility:** Reflect on your comfort level and trust in their guidance. Your estate planning attorney will handle sensitive matters, so you should feel confident in their expertise and comfortable with their approach.

The Elephant in the Room: Discussing Fees and Costs

No one likes to talk about this subject, but it just might be the most important. Discussing fees and costs with a prospective estate planning attorney is often the elephant in the room, but transparent conversations about costs can establish trust and ensure that there are no surprises down the line. The following are some strategies to navigate it effectively:

Be Upfront: Initiate the conversation about fees early on. Asking directly about billing practices, fee structures (flat fee, hourly rate, etc.), and what those fees include can set clear expectations from the start.

Understand the Full Scope: Inquire about all potential costs associated with your estate planning. This includes not only the attorney's fees but also any additional costs for filing fees, costs for appraisals, or charges for consulting outside experts.

Ask for a Written Estimate: Requesting a written estimate or a fee agreement can provide a tangible reference for the discussed services and their costs.

Negotiate When Appropriate: While not all fees are negotiable, asking if some packages or alternatives could reduce costs doesn't hurt.

Discuss Payment Options: Explore payment options or plans that the attorney might offer. Some firms may provide flexibility in how and when fees are paid, which can ease financial pressure.

Utilizing Free & Low-Cost Legal Resources

Guide to Free Legal Advice Resources

The adage "the best things in life are free" can sometimes apply in estate planning. There's a treasure trove of resources offering no-cost guidance to help you navigate the often-complex world of wills, trusts, and estate planning. **Here's a quick guide to some reliable organizations and platforms with which you can access free legal advice:**

- **Legal Aid Societies:** Across the country, these organizations provide free legal services to those who qualify, typically based on income. Legal aid societies can offer basic estate planning advice, help with drafting simple wills, and provide guidance on powers of attorney and healthcare directives.

- **American Bar Association (ABA):** The ABA offers various resources, including a directory of pro bono programs, where you can find free legal assistance for estate planning.

- **Law School Clinics:** Many law schools operate legal clinics where students, supervised by licensed attorneys, offer free legal services to the community. These can be an excellent resource for estate planning.

- **Online Legal Platforms:** Websites like Nolo and the Legal Services Corporation (LSC) offer articles, templates, and tools to help with DIY estate planning. While they don't replace personalized legal advice, they can provide some helpful knowledge.

Low-Cost Legal Aid Services

Inexpensive (or less pricey) legal aid services can make estate planning accessible for everyone, not just those with deep pockets. Non-profit organizations and legal aid societies across the US offer vital services—from will drafting to more complex advice—at reduced or no cost.

Finding these services usually starts with a bit of homework to locate a nearby legal aid provider, many of which receive support from the LSC. While income often determines eligibility, with services aimed at lower-income individuals, many legal aid organizations also account for other circumstances, offering help based on a sliding scale.

Special consideration is often given to seniors, veterans, or those with disabilities, acknowledging their specific estate-planning needs. To explore what's available, reach out to local legal aid with your financial details ready.

Free Online Legal Information Sources

Thankfully, the digital age brings a wealth of information right to our fingertips. Free online legal resources can be valuable for those beginning their estate planning, offering insights into the basics of wills, trusts, powers of attorney, and more. **Below are some recommended websites to initiate your self-education:**

1. **Nolo:** Renowned for its do-it-yourself legal guides, Nolo offers many articles on estate planning that clearly explain legal terms and processes. It's a great starting point for anyone new to the topic.

2. **Legal Information Institute (LII) at Cornell Law School:** This resource provides free access to a wide range of legal information, including an overview of estate-planning laws, making complex legal doctrines more digestible.

3. **The American Bar Association (ABA):** The ABA's website features consumer-friendly guides on estate planning, including tips on choosing an attorney and understanding your legal rights and obligations.

4. **Find Law:** This website offers extensive articles on estate planning, including step-by-step guides on how to create a will, set up trusts, and navigate probate.

Utilizing Pro Bono Services for Estate Planning

Tapping into pro bono services for estate planning can provide legal assistance without the financial strain. Pro bono, meaning "for the public good," involves legal professionals offering their services free of charge to those unable to afford them.

Qualifying for Pro Bono Services: Typically, eligibility for pro bono assistance hinges on income level, often targeting individuals or families with incomes at or below the poverty line. However, many organizations also consider other factors, such as age, disability, or veteran status. Contact local legal aid societies or non-profit organizations specializing in estate planning who can guide you through eligibility and connect you with available resources.

Finding Pro Bono Services: Legal clinics at law schools, bar associations, and public interest law organizations are prime sources for pro bono support. Many have specific programs for estate planning, offering everything from basic will drafting to more complex estate-management advice.

- **Advantages:** The most obvious benefit is cost savings, making legal advice accessible for estate planning. Additionally, pro bono services can clarify legal jargon and processes, allowing individuals to make informed decisions about their estates.

- **Limitations:** While pro bono services are helpful, they may have limitations. Resources can be stretched thin, which can then lead to wait times. Also, the scope of services might be limited, focusing on basic estate planning rather than more nuanced or complex scenarios.

Key Takeaways

1. **Know Your Options:** Understand the different fee structures, such as flat fees, hourly rates, and contingency fees, and how they impact your estate planning budget. This knowledge helps you make informed decisions about hiring legal help.

2. **DIY Can Work, But With Caution:** DIY estate planning is feasible for simpler estates, but be aware of the risks. Missteps like failing to properly execute documents can lead to costly errors.

3. **Tech Is Your Friend:** Online tools and resources can simplify the estate-planning process, making it more accessible. Always verify that these tools are up to date with current laws to avoid potential pitfalls.

4. **Preparation Saves Money:** Being organized and clear about your estate-planning goals before consulting a lawyer can reduce billable

hours. Gather all necessary documents and questions in advance to maximize the efficiency of legal consultations.

5. **Negotiation Is Possible:** Don't be afraid to discuss and negotiate legal fees with your attorney. Understanding the scope of work and asking about alternative billing arrangements can lead to more favorable terms.

6. **Pro Bono and Low-Cost Resources:** For those unable to afford traditional legal fees, exploring pro bono services, low-cost legal aid, and free online legal resources can provide assistance without breaking the bank.

Chapter 5

The Great Debate Between Wills and Trusts

"In the end, it's not the years in your life that count. It's the life in your years."
-Abraham Lincoln, 16th President of the United States

Wills: A Breakdown

Estate planning begins with understanding the foundational tools, and wills are the first step. A will, simply put, is a document that details what you want regarding the distribution of your assets and care of dependents after you pass away. The blueprint outlines how you want your legacy to be managed, making it the core of estate planning.

Lasting Impressions: The Role of a Will in Your Estate Plan

A will ensures that your wishes are legally recognized and fulfilled. It can guide your loved ones on handling your assets, caring for your children, and even managing personal sentiments after you've moved on.

This document is your opportunity to lay it all out—everything from who you want to inherit your collectibles to who should take over the reins of your business. It also spells out who you trust to raise your kids if you can't raise them yourself. Without a will, you're leaving these decisions up to state laws.

Having a will means taking control and making sure that your estate is divided precisely how you see fit. It's about putting your stamp on the future and ensuring that your legacy is shaped according to your values and wishes. Essentially, a will ensures that your life's work is honored, your loved ones are cared for, and your final wishes are heard and legally upheld.

Key Components & Legal Requirements of Wills

A will must have key components to be considered valid and enforceable. First, it must clearly identify the person creating the will (the **testator**) and state unequivocally that the document is intended to serve their wishes.

A will should also appoint an **executor** to carry out what you intended. The executor steers the will through probate, so choosing this person is important. Additionally, a will needs to detail the distribution of assets—from the family home to the smallest sentimental items—specifying who gets what.

Beneficiaries, those who'll inherit the assets, must be clearly named. Minor children need a guardian appointed in the will to ensure that they're taken care of by a trusted adult.

Legal requirements for wills can vary by state, including the need for witnesses during the signing. Some states accept "holographic" (handwritten) wills, while others have stricter rules. Regardless of where you live, your will needs to meet state-specific legal requirements to be fully valid.

The Perils of Informal Promises: Marlon Brando's Legacy

Despite legendary actor Marlon Brando's intentions to provide for his longtime housekeeper, Angela Borlaza, through a verbal promise of homeownership, the absence of a formal inclusion in his will led to a lawsuit after he died in 2004. Borlaza claimed that Brando had promised her the house she lived in, but the estate challenged her claim, leading to a legal battle that was eventually settled out of court.

This situation underscores the importance of legally and formally documenting all estate-related promises and intentions. It also highlights the potential for disputes when relying on verbal agreements or promises not backed by legal documentation.

Family Complexities: Choosing Direct & Alternate Beneficiaries

Beneficiary designations can feel complex, especially in families where relationships and circumstances might be varied. In your estate plan, selecting direct beneficiaries (those who'll inherit your assets) is a task that requires careful thought and, often, a delicate balance of family dynamics.

It's not just about choosing who gets what. It's equally important to designate alternate beneficiaries. These are the backups, the plan B, for situations in which your primary choice cannot inherit, whether due to passing away before you, incapacity, or simply choosing not to accept the inheritance.

Including alternate beneficiaries can help ensure that your assets don't end up in unintended hands or become subject to the probate process unnecessarily.

Probate: What Is It? Why Do You Want to Avoid It?

Probate is like the DMV of the afterlife for your assets. It's where your estate goes to get sorted out under the watchful eyes of the court before anything gets passed on to your heirs. It's a legal process that authenticates your will and oversees your assets' distribution, ensuring that debts and taxes are paid off first. While it sounds straightforward, probate can be a slow, public, and often expensive ride that many prefer to skip.

The downsides? Time, for starters. Probate can stretch out for months or even years, delaying when your loved ones can receive their inheritance. Then there's the cost, with attorney and court fees eating into what you've left behind. Also, probate records are public, meaning that anyone curious enough can peek into the details of your estate.

Often, there are ways for estate-planning strategies to bypass probate altogether, like setting up trusts or designating beneficiaries on accounts. While this chapter gives you a primer on probate, we'll dive deeper into how to avoid it later on in the book, equipping you with strategies to ensure that your estate goes directly to those you intend without the extra hassle or expense.

Finding Samples of Types of Wills

The internet is the easiest place to start if you'd like to see examples of what a will should encompass. From simple wills for straightforward estates to more complex ones that account for various assets and family dynamics, there's likely a template or sample that somewhat matches your needs. Legal websites, estate planning software, and even some government and non-profit organizations offer these resources, often with guidelines on how to fill them out.

Below are a few that might be a good fit:

- **LegalZoom:** This online legal services company provides will templates that can be customized to fit individual needs. They also offer guidance on how to complete these documents properly.

- **Nolo:** A long-established provider of legal guides and forms, Nolo's website offers will templates that can be purchased and downloaded.

- **Rocket Lawyer:** This platform offers legal documents, including will templates, with the option for consultation with attorneys. Rocket Lawyer's documents can also be tailored to your specific state's laws.

- **US Legal Wills:** Specializing in wills and estate planning, US Legal Wills offers an online tool that guides users through the process of creating a will.

- **DoYourOwnWill:** As the name suggests, this free resource provides users with the tools to create their own wills online.

However, finding a will template is just the start. A template might cover the basics, but every estate and family is different, and so customization is key. This might involve tweaking the distribution of assets, adding specific guardianship clauses for minor children, or incorporating trusts for more complex estates.

While these templates can be a great starting point, they're most effective when used as a draft to be reviewed and refined by a legal professional.

Trusts: Different Types & Their Purposes

The Many Reasons You May Need a Trust

Trusts[7] are versatile tools equipped to handle various situations. Their advantages are numerous, catering to specific needs that a will alone might not address. As we've touched upon earlier, trusts offer a sophisticated approach to managing and protecting your assets during and after your lifetime.

One of the biggest advantages of a trust is its ability to bypass probate, facilitating a smoother transfer of assets to beneficiaries. Unlike the contents of a will, which become public records through probate, trusts keep your financial affairs out of public records.

Trusts also offer flexibility for your asset distributions. Whether you want to set aside funds for a child's education, provide for a loved one with special needs without affecting their eligibility for government assistance, or stagger inheritances to ensure financial maturity, trusts can be tailored to meet these specific requirements.

They can also provide large tax advantages, which can reduce estate and gift taxes. In addition, trusts also offer protection for your assets from creditors and legal judgments against beneficiaries, ensuring that your legacy reaches your heirs as intended.

Understanding Different Types of Trusts

Trusts come in many forms, so here's a brief overview of some of the more common types:

---

[7] https://www.thebalancemoney.com/what-is-a-trust-fund-357254

Revocable[8] Living Trust: Often used for avoiding probate, this trust can be altered or dissolved by the trustmaker during their lifetime. It's a flexible option that allows you to retain control over your assets while living. At death, your assets will transfer to your beneficiaries.

Irrevocable Trust: As the name suggests, this trust will be difficult to change after it's in place. It offers benefits like protection from creditors and estate tax advantages because the assets in the trust aren't considered in your personal estate any longer.

Testamentary Trust: This trust is created as part of a will and only comes into effect after the trustmaker's death. It's helpful in managing assets for beneficiaries over time, rather than distributing everything outright.

Charitable Trust: Ideal for those who wish to support charitable causes, this can provide tax benefits while also allowing you to specify how your assets are used for philanthropic efforts.

Special Needs Trust: Designed to benefit someone with disabilities, the intention is to set up this trust without hindering their eligibility for government assistance and ensuring that they're provided for without jeopardizing their benefits.

How Trusts Operate & Who's Involved

Trusts operate on a framework that involves specific roles, each with distinct responsibilities, so that the trust's objectives are met efficiently and legally. Understanding who's involved and how a trust operates provides clarity and structure to this essential estate planning tool.

---

[8] https://smartasset.com/retirement/what-is-a-revocable-living-trust

- **Settlor (or Grantor):** This is the creator of the trust who decides how the assets should be managed and distributed. The settlor sets the terms of the trust, choosing beneficiaries and appointing trustees while laying the groundwork for how the trust will function.

- **Trustee:** The trustee is the heart of trust administration and is tasked with managing the trust's assets according to the settlor's instructions. This role involves investing assets wisely, distributing them to beneficiaries, and ensuring that the trust complies with legal and tax obligations. Trustees can be individuals (a trusted friend or family member) or institutions (such as a bank or trust company).

- **Beneficiaries:** These are the individuals or entities who'll benefit from the trust. Beneficiaries may receive income or principal from the trust based on the terms set by the settlor.

The process of trust administration begins with the trustee taking control of the trust assets, followed by the ongoing management of those assets. This includes investing funds, making distributions as dictated by the trust terms, and performing any necessary reporting or tax filings. Trustees are burdened with the fiduciary duty, which means that they must act in the best interest of the beneficiaries only.

Trust Fund Baby: The Impact of Trusts on Beneficiaries & Heirs

The term "trust fund baby" often conjures up images of wealth and privilege, but the reality is that many people who aren't rich have trusts as well. As financial tools, trusts profoundly impact beneficiaries and heirs, shaping their futures significantly. Beyond clichés, trusts can offer protection, support, and a foundation for growth. Still, they're also responsible for balancing these benefits with promoting independence and personal development.

Trusts can provide for education, healthcare, and general welfare, ensuring that beneficiaries have the necessary resources to succeed. They can protect assets from external threats like creditors or divorce settlements, ensuring that wealth is preserved for future generations. This protective shield allows heirs to take calculated risks, such as starting a business or pursuing a non-traditional career path, knowing that they have a financial safety net.

However, the challenge lies in structuring trusts to support beneficiaries without stifling their motivation or sense of responsibility. Trusts can be tailored with stipulations encouraging beneficiaries to achieve personal milestones, such as completing an education or working in a chosen field, before gaining access to substantial assets. This approach helps in building a sense of accomplishment and self-reliance among heirs.

When done right, trusts can ensure financial security while encouraging personal growth and independence, leaving a lasting and positive legacy for future generations.

The Million Dollar Question: Will, Trust, or Both?

Assessing the Pros & Cons of Wills & Trusts

Wills and trusts each offer distinct advantages and challenges, and so understanding their differences can help craft a plan that best aligns with your objectives.

Wills are often celebrated for their simplicity and directness—they allow you to state your wishes for asset distribution and the guardianship of minors after you pass away. They're relatively easy and less expensive to create, but they also must go through probate.

On the other hand, trusts offer a more complex solution with the benefit of avoiding probate, thus providing privacy and potentially reducing estate taxes and legal costs. Trusts can be used to manage your assets during and after your lifetime, offering greater control over when and how your assets are distributed.

However, trusts require more upfront work and expense to establish and maintain. They demand a comprehensive transfer of assets into the trust and ongoing management, which can be seen as a disadvantage for those seeking a simpler estate plan.

Ultimately, the choice between a will and a trust—or the decision to use both—depends on your specific estate planning goals and the complexity of your assets, as well as your desires for privacy, control, and ease of transfer to your heirs.

Scenarios In Which Both Wills and Trusts are Beneficial

Sometimes, estate planning requires intertwining the structured steps of wills with the strategic flows of trusts. This combined approach ensures that your estate planning needs are covered and addresses scenarios that might not work with either tool alone.

One common situation that benefits from this dual strategy is when you have minor children. A will can appoint guardians for their care, a deeply personal decision and not typically addressed within a trust. Concurrently, a trust can manage the assets you leave for those children, ensuring that they're used as you've specified until they reach an appropriate age.

Another scenario involves specific assets you wish to pass outside of probate. While a will covers the breadth of your estate, a trust can immediately transfer certain assets upon death, bypassing the time consuming and public probate process. This is particularly beneficial for privacy-conscious individuals or when aiming to provide for a spouse or dependent without legal delays.

Additionally, for those with complex assets, including businesses, real estate in multiple states, or significant philanthropic wishes, employing both wills and trusts allows nuanced control over different parts of the estate. This ensures that each asset is handled advantageously, whether through the direct simplicity of a will or the detailed provisions of a trust.

Hidden Costs: Financial Implications of Wills & Trusts

Wills and trusts are about preparing your assets for when you're gone but also about understanding and preparing for the hidden costs associated with each option. These aren't just the fees for drawing up the documents—there can be ongoing expenses that can nibble away at an estate if not planned for carefully.

With wills, the primary hidden cost is often probate, the court process to validate the will and oversee the distribution of the estate. Probate can be lengthy and expensive, with legal fees, court costs, and executor fees reducing the estate's value. Conversely, trusts, particularly living trusts, generally bypass probate, but they're not free from costs either. Setting up a trust is typically more expensive upfront than drafting a will, and there can be ongoing management fees, especially if you appoint a professional trustee.

Furthermore, both wills and trusts may involve tax implications. Trusts, for instance, can be structured to minimize estate taxes, but the setup and maintenance require a further understanding of tax laws to capitalize on these benefits.

A Legal Thriller: The Estate of Tom Clancy

The story of Tom Clancy, the bestselling author known for his military-themed novels, is definitely one to be aware of. Clancy died in 2013 and left behind an estate valued at around $86 million. Despite having an estate plan, Clancy's will led to a legal battle among his family members that lasted for years, primarily due to ambiguities around how the estate's taxes should be divided between his wife and the children from a previous marriage.

The heart of the dispute was a codicil (an amendment to his will) made to Clancy's estate plan just months before his death. This amendment led to confusion over whether his widow or his children from his previous marriage were responsible for the hefty estate taxes. The lack of clarity in the document's wording resulted in a prolonged court case, which could've been mitigated with more precise language and, perhaps, more thorough estate-planning tools like trusts that would've offered clearer directives.

Considering Time Factors in Wills & Trusts

Timing is central to ensuring that your wills and trusts do exactly what you intend them to do. The effectiveness of these documents isn't set in stone once you complete them—it evolves with your life's milestones and the changing legal landscape.

In simple terms, wills and trusts aren't one-and-done deals. They're more like living documents that need to grow and adapt with you. For instance, major life events such as marriage, childbirth, divorce, or the acquisition of significant assets likely warrant a review and possibly an update to your estate plan to reflect your current wishes and circumstances.

Moreover, laws governing wills, trusts, and estates are never static. They can and do change, sometimes significantly. Staying current on these changes is important because what worked perfectly under one set of laws might not under another. A trust set up in one legal environment might need adjustments to remain effective or to take advantage of new opportunities for tax savings or asset protection offered by updated laws.

The Final Verdict: Making an Informed Decision

The decision regarding whether a will, a trust, or a combination of both best suits your needs is deeply personal and hinges on a thorough understanding of your estate planning goals.

Consider wills and trusts not as competing options but rather as complementary tools in your estate planning. A will is straightforward and cost-effective for appointing guardians for minors, but it comes with the probate process. Trusts, while more complex and initially costly, offer privacy, flexibility, and can save time and money in the long run by avoiding probate.

Life changes—from marriages and births to acquisitions or losses, as well as law updates, may necessitate a flexible and adaptable estate plan. Regularly reviewing and updating your estate documents ensures that your plan evolves with you and reflects your wishes.

Making an informed decision generally requires professional guidance. Estate planning attorneys provide strategic advice, tailor plans to your needs, and anticipate scenarios that you may not have considered. Their expertise is hugely valuable in navigating estate law's complexities and making choices that secure your legacy as intended.

Key Takeaways

1. **Understanding the Essentials:** Recognizing the role of wills and their legal requirements in estate planning ensures that your estate is managed and distributed according to your wishes.

2. **Navigating Family Dynamics:** Addressing family complexities through careful designation of direct and alternate beneficiaries in wills mitigates potential disputes and ensures that your assets are distributed as intended.

3. **The Value of Trusts:** Exploring the various types of trusts underscores their versatility and strategic value in estate planning. Trusts offer tailored solutions for asset management, protection, and transfer, providing significant benefits beyond the capabilities of wills alone.

4. **Comprehensive Planning with Wills and Trusts[9]:** Evaluating the advantages and disadvantages of wills versus trusts highlights the importance of a comprehensive approach. In many scenarios, integrating both wills and trusts into your estate plan can offer the most effective solution for achieving your estate planning goals.

5. **Anticipating Hidden Costs:** Being mindful of the hidden costs associated with wills and trusts encourages proactive planning.

6. **Adapting to Changes:** Acknowledging the impact of timing and life changes on the effectiveness of wills and trusts emphasizes the need for regular updates. Stay informed about legal updates and adjust your estate plan accordingly.

---

[9] https://preserveyourestate.net/blog/wills-and-trusts/5-reasons-wills-arent-sufficient-estate-plan/

Chapter 6

Live Long & Prosper: Planning for Your Retirement

"For retirement, the formula is simple:
spend less than you make and invest the difference wisely."
-Warren Buffett, American business tycoon and legendary philanthropist

Estate Planning & Your Retirement: The Connection

Retirement requires planning, and so integrating estate planning and retirement strategies will transition your legacy and financial security for your golden years. This section explores the relationship between estate planning and retirement, highlighting how each influences and strengthens the other.

Ties That Bind: How Estate Planning & Retirement Planning Intersect

When mapping out your future, think of estate and retirement planning as two peas in a pod, as they absolutely go hand in hand. It's all about making sure that you've got a solid game plan, ensuring that what you've worked hard for benefits you throughout retirement and then smoothly transitions to your loved ones when the time comes.

As we've established, estate planning is ensuring that your wishes are clearly known, legally documented, and easily executed, covering everything from who gets your prized collections to who looks after your finances if you can't. On the flipside, retirement planning is about making sure that you can live comfortably without worrying about your financial stability once you decide to slow down.

When these two plans work together, they create a harmony that secures your golden years and safeguards your legacy. It all comes down to balancing enjoying your retirement to the fullest and ensuring that your loved ones are cared for as you envision. By integrating these plans, you're covering your bases and allowing all aspects of your financial life to be in tune with your goals and values.

Strategic Legacy: Johnny Carson's Approach to Estate and Retirement Planning

Johnny Carson, the iconic host of "The Tonight Show," was known for his private nature that extended into how he managed his estate and retirement planning. Carson was proactive in his estate planning, ensuring that his assets were structured to maximize benefits for his heirs while minimizing taxes and potential legal complications. His use of trusts to manage his assets is a testament to the strategic integration of estate and retirement planning.

This story highlights how Carson's approach to retirement planning, including using trusts, protected his privacy and ensured a smooth transition of his wealth to his beneficiaries.

Beneficiary Designations: Ensuring That Your Assets End Up in the Right Place

Imagine you've got a roadmap for where you want your assets to go after you're gone. That's where beneficiary designations come into play, which you can think of as your assets' GPS, guiding them directly to the people you choose. These designations are important in your retirement and estate plans, ensuring that your 401(k), life insurance, and savings account earmarked for your grandkid's college fund land exactly where you intend.

Getting these designations right ensures that your wishes are heard loud and clear, bypassing the more public and sometimes messy probate process. It's a direct express lane for your assets and cuts through potential legal red tape. But if your beneficiary information isn't up to date or, worse, is missing, your assets might take a detour and can end up in the hands of someone you hadn't planned on.

It's about sitting down and making sure that every account, policy, and plan has the right name attached. Changing these names as life fluctuates (think marriage, divorce, or new family members) ensures that your assets don't just wander aimlessly but instead reach the people you've chosen.

Living Trusts & Retirement: A Match Made in Heaven?

These two things might just be the perfect pair. At the heart of their harmony is how living trusts can complement and enhance your retirement planning, providing a seamless transition of assets and ensuring that your golden years are as smooth as possible.

A living trust allows for you to control your assets while you're alive and well, with the added benefit of transferring them directly to your beneficiaries upon your passing, bypassing the costly and time-consuming probate process. This means that more of your assets go directly to your family without the wait or the public scrutiny that comes with probate.

Moreover, living trusts offer flexibility that's particularly valuable in retirement. For example, if you become incapacitated, a successor trustee you've named can manage your affairs without needing a court-appointed guardian. This protects your privacy and autonomy, and it also makes sure that your assets continue to be managed as you intended, with both security and peace of mind.

Minimizing Taxes: Strategies for Your Retirement and Estate

Picture this: You've spent years filling your retirement and estate coffers, only to see a chunk of it whittled away by taxes. Not the ideal scenario in the slightest, but that's where smart tax strategies come into play. They serve as the financial savvy that keeps more of your hard-earned money in your pocket and, eventually, in the hands of your loved ones.

You need to understand which accounts to tap into first to keep your tax bills low. For instance, knowing the ins and outs of Roth IRAs versus traditional IRAs can make a substantial difference in your tax obligations during retirement. Similarly, when you're eyeing estate planning, gifting assets when you're alive or setting up trusts can reduce the estate tax hit, with more wealth transitions according to your wishes.

The trick is to weave these strategies together, crafting a plan in which your retirement savings support you comfortably through your golden years and pass on efficiently to your beneficiaries. Working with a financial advisor to build these strategies can make all the difference, turning tax planning from a dreaded task into a key component of your financial legacy.

A Legacy of Giving: Kirk Kerkorian's Philanthropic Estate Planning

American businessman Kirk Kerkorian was one of the most influential figures in the development of Las Vegas. Kerkorian was known for his investments in the automotive and airline industries, and especially for his significant contributions to the Las Vegas casino scene. Despite his vast wealth, Kerkorian was also recognized for his discreet philanthropy and careful planning regarding his estate and retirement. Through his charitable organization, The Lincy Foundation, he's made donations of more than $1 billion, with nothing named in his honor.

Kerkorian's estate planning was notably strategic, incorporating various aspects of his extensive portfolio to ensure that his philanthropic goals continued after he died in 2015. He established a trust that secured his legacy and detailed the distribution of his assets to various charitable causes. His retirement planning was seamlessly integrated with his estate planning, ensuring that his assets were protected and utilized according to his wishes, both during retirement and posthumously.

Building Your Nest Egg: Investment Strategies for Retirement

Playing the Long Game: Understanding Long-Term Investments

Embracing long-term investing is the only way to really plan for retirement, as time really is your ally. Long-term investments, such as stocks, bonds, mutual funds, and exchange-traded funds, have the potential to weather the ups and downs of market volatility and gradually build wealth over decades.

The reason for this comes down to the power of compounding, as the returns on your investments make their own returns. Over time, this effect can turn modest savings into huge gains. It requires patience, discipline, and a forward-looking mindset, steering clear of the temptation to react hastily to short-term market fluctuations.

Moreover, long-term investing often allows you to diversify your portfolio with many asset classes. This diversification spreads risk, reducing the impact of subpar performance in a single investment to your overall portfolio.

Understanding and committing to long-term investing is a surefire method to securing your financial future. Invest early, invest often, and invest as much as possible to have the retirement you've always dreamed of.

The Importance of a Diverse Portfolio

Diversifying your investment portfolio lies in spreading your investments across various asset classes such as stocks, bonds, real estate, and perhaps even commodities or precious metals. This strategy makes your portfolio more efficient, generating more returns over time per unit of risk taken. Ensuring proper diversification is step #1 in investing.

Just as you wouldn't wear a raincoat as your only protection in all weather conditions, relying on a single type of investment exposes you to unnecessary risks. Market volatility can affect asset classes differently at different times. By diversifying, you ensure that a downturn in one sector won't capsize your entire financial plan. Instead, losses in one area can be offset by gains in another, stabilizing your portfolio's overall performance.

Moreover, a diverse portfolio allows you to take advantage of the varying growth rates of different investments. While some assets might offer steady, modest returns, others might present the opportunity for significant growth, balancing the pursuit of long-term security with the potential for outsized return.

Realistic Risks & Rewards in Your Retirement Investments

Finding the sweet spot between chasing gains and security is difficult when investing. It's all about striking a balance that lets you sleep soundly at night while your investments work hard in the background. This equilibrium is important because your golden years should be about enjoying life and not fretting over stock tickers.

The potential for high returns usually means that you have to increase the risk. On the flipside, ultra-safe investments are like taking the scenic route at a leisurely pace. It's less risky but it might take you longer to get where you want to go, and the returns may be lower overall.

The main factor is you need to assess your risk tolerance and retirement timeline. If you've got years to go before you hang up your work boots (or dress shoes), you might be able to afford a few bumps along the way, aiming for higher returns. But shifting gears toward more secure investments can protect your nest egg from market downturns as you get closer to retirement. Remember—a well-balanced portfolio doesn't eliminate risk altogether but it *can* help you manage it, ensuring that your retirement savings are there for you when you need them most.

With investing, it's generally advisable to get professional advice, especially if you're unfamiliar with how investing works.

Compounding: Retirement Savings Can Grow with Time

Compounding is the key to long-term investing, turning time into your greatest financial ally. This financial phenomenon occurs when the earnings on your investments start generating their own earnings. In simpler terms, it's like planting a tree and then watching as its seeds plant more trees, exponentially expanding your forest over time.

The earlier you start saving and investing, the more potent the compounding effect becomes. Even modest amounts saved in your 20s or 30s can grow into significant sums by retirement, thanks to the repeated cycle of earning interest on your interest. As they say, the best day to invest is the day you are born, and the second best day is today.

Compounding emphasizes the importance of consistent, early investment in retirement accounts such as IRAs or 401(k)s. By continuously contributing to these accounts over several decades, you allow your investments the maximum amount of time to grow and benefit from the compounding effect. Run some numbers in an online financial planning calculator to get a real idea of how this works.

For example, if you have $50,000 saved and invest $500 monthly, in 20 years at 5% compound interest (annually) you'll have $331,060.61. This is despite only contributing $170,000 total. However, if you run those same numbers but for 30 years instead, you'll end up with $614,730.20, despite only investing $230,000. That compound interest makes a *huge* difference!

Leveraging Your Social Security & Pension Plans

Social Security 101: Understanding the Basics

Social Security is one of the pillars of retirement planning. Think of it as a faithful companion, quietly tagging along during your working years and ready to step in with support when you decide to slow down. Funded by payroll taxes, the program is designed to provide retirees, disabled individuals, and survivors with a steady income stream.

In a nutshell, the amount you receive depends on how long you've worked, how much you've earned, and when you choose to start collecting benefits. A bit of strategy is involved, as claiming benefits at the earliest age of 62 will give you more checks, but they'll be smaller. If you wait until your full retirement age, you'll receive a larger monthly amount. Hold off even longer (up to age 70) and your checks get a significant boost, thanks to delayed retirement credits.

So how do you make Social Security work best for you? It starts with understanding your financial needs in retirement and considering how other savings and investments fit into the picture. Consulting with a financial advisor to navigate your Social Security options can help you maximize this benefit to support your retirement lifestyle.

Pension Plan Playbook: How to Make the Most of Your Pension

If you're lucky enough to have a pension plan[10], consider it a key piece in your retirement, offering a reliable income stream in your retirement years.

First, get to know your plan. Is it a defined benefit, promising a specific payout at retirement based on salary and years of service? Or is it a defined contribution plan, in which the payout depends on how much is contributed and how investments perform? Understanding the rules and benefits of your plan is your first step.

Next, you need to consider when you'll start taking your pension. Some plans offer the options to start early at a reduced rate or to delay for a larger payout. It's a balance between immediate needs and future gains.

Also, consider survivor benefits. If you have a partner, how will your pension decision affect them? Some plans offer options to provide for a spouse after your death, which could influence your choice.

---

[10] https://www.investopedia.com/terms/p/pensionplan.asp

Making the most of your pension means considering your overall retirement strategy and sometimes consulting with a financial advisor to ensure that your moves are perfectly timed for a secure retirement.

Timing is Everything: When to Start Drawing Social Security & Pensions

Deciding when to tap into Social Security and pension benefits can make a big difference in how much you receive overall. With retirement benefits, timing isn't just about age—it's also about maximizing what you've worked hard to accumulate and ensuring that you have a comfortable and sustained flow of income throughout your retirement years.

For Social Security, the magic numbers are 62 (early retirement), your full retirement age (somewhere between 66 and 67 for most people), and 70 (the age at which benefits max out). Claiming benefits at 62 might be tempting, but it reduces your monthly check. Waiting until your full retirement age or, even better, until you're 70, can significantly increase your monthly benefit, offering more financial comfort as you age. Longevity is the biggest factor here.

Pensions have their own set of timing considerations. Some plans might allow you to start collecting early at a reduced rate, while others might increase your payout if you delay. The choice often depends on your financial needs, health status, and whether you have other income sources to support you should you choose to hold off.

In both cases, it's about looking at the big picture and making a strategic choice that aligns with your overall retirement plan. Consulting with a financial advisor can help you with these decisions and ensure that you're making the best timing choice regarding your retirement income.

Safety Nets: Understanding Survivor & Disability Benefits

These are the safety nets that catch you and your loved ones in the case of unforeseen events. These benefits are crucial to a well-rounded retirement strategy and make certain that financial security continues even when life throws curveballs.

Survivor benefits, for instance, are a lifeline for the family members you might leave behind. If Social Security covers you or you have a pension, understanding how these benefits extend to your spouse, children, or dependents is key. It's about making sure that they're not left in a financial lurch if you're no longer around. For many, it provides a less stressful environment knowing that loved ones will have a financial backup when you pass away.

Disability benefits, on the other hand, are there to support you if an injury or illness prevents you from working before you hit retirement. Often overlooked in retirement planning, these benefits can be a game changer in maintaining your quality of life and financial independence during tough times.

Incorporating both into your retirement strategy means looking beyond the golden years to ensure that you and your family are covered no matter what. It's about asking the right questions now, like "What coverage do I have, and what do my loved ones need?" so that you can confidently navigate the future.

Considering Healthcare Costs in Retirement

The Price of Longevity: Projecting Healthcare Costs in Retirement

We all hope to ride the wave of longevity, but there's a price tag attached. Especially when it comes to healthcare in retirement, our bodies need a bit more tuning and maintenance as we age, and the cost of that upkeep can be more than just pocket change. Preparing for the inevitable rise in health care expenses can help ensure that your retirement savings don't hit a snag when you need them most.

Think of health care costs as an investment in your future self. Just as you'd save for a dream vacation or a grandchild's education, setting aside funds for medical expenses is planning for the quality of life you deserve. Whether for regular check-ups, prescription medications, or more significant health interventions, these costs can add up quickly and make a noticeable dent in your retirement savings.

The trick is to start early. Consider options like health savings accounts (HSAs) that offer tax advantages, or investing in a health insurance plan that caters to retirees. Understanding Medicare and supplemental insurance can also help you navigate the maze of health care financing. And don't forget that financial advisors can often help in this area, too.

What To Know About Medicare & Medicaid

Each has its own set of rules and benefits, and so understanding these programs will help to cover health care costs in retirement without running through your retirement savings.

Medicare, the main health care provider for those 65 and older, offers a range of coverage options, from hospital stays (Part A) to outpatient services (Part B) and even prescription drugs (Part D). But remember that there are premiums, deductibles, and co-pays to consider.

Medicaid, on the other hand, is for individuals with limited income and resources. It can fill in the gaps that Medicare leaves and cover additional services like long-term care, which Medicare typically doesn't. Eligibility for Medicaid varies by state and requires going through a lot of paperwork, so it's best to use a professional service to help you.

Yay or Nay on Long-Term Care Insurance?

Deciding on long-term care insurance is difficult because it's expensive, but if you need it, you'll be glad that you're prepared. As we age, the likelihood of needing some form of long-term care increases, whether that's in-home assistance, adult day care, or a stay in a nursing home. These services can quickly drain retirement savings, making long-term care insurance an option worth considering.

Long-term care insurance provides a safety net, covering costs that Medicare or private health insurance typically doesn't. It's more for peace of mind and ensuring that you can afford the care you might need without sacrificing your or your family's financial security. However, it's not a one-size-fits-all solution—premiums can be pricey and they often increase over time. Also, there's the gamble of paying for something that you may never use.

So is it a yay or nay? It boils down to your personal risk tolerance, financial situation, and health history. Evaluating your need for long-term care insurance involves closely examining your retirement savings, potential care costs, and how much of a financial impact you're willing to bear. For many, it's a calculated decision to protect against the high costs of long-term care and ensuring that a rainy day doesn't wash away their financial security.

What Health Savings Accounts Can Do for You

Health savings accounts (HSAs) offer a triple tax advantage—contributions are tax-deductible, earnings grow tax-free, and withdrawals for qualified medical expenses aren't taxed. This makes HSAs an invaluable tool in affordably managing health care costs during your retirement years.

When you contribute to an HSA, you set aside pre-tax dollars to pay for future medical expenses. This can include visits to the doctor and prescriptions to dental work and long-term care services. The beauty of HSAs lies not just in their immediate tax benefits but also in their potential for long-term growth. Funds in an HSA can be invested, much like those in a retirement account, allowing them to grow over the years.

One of the best features of HSAs is their flexibility. Unlike flexible spending accounts (FSAs), there's no "use it or lose it" policy. Unspent funds roll over year after year, making HSAs an excellent way to save for health care costs in retirement. Moreover, after reaching age 65, you can withdraw funds for non-medical expenses without penalty, although these withdrawals will be taxed as income.

Key Takeaways

1. **Integrating Estate and Retirement Planning:** Understand how these two very different things can work hand in hand. Planning for both simultaneously ensures a comprehensive approach to securing your financial future and legacy.

2. **The Significance of Beneficiary Designations:** Regularly update beneficiary designations for both your insurance policies and your retirement accounts. It typically bypasses the probate process and can help transition the assets the way you intended them to.

3. **Advantages of Living Trusts in Retirement Planning:** Living trusts can be a strategic part of retirement planning, offering benefits like avoiding probate and providing more control over asset distribution.

4. **Tax Efficiency Strategies:** Employing strategies to minimize taxes on retirement income and estate transmission can significantly impact your financial legacy, maximizing the benefits for you and your heirs.

5. **The Role of Long-Term Investments and Diverse Portfolios:** Emphasizing long-term investments and maintaining a diverse portfolio is key to balancing potential gains with security.

6. **Health Care Costs and Insurance Options:** Planning for health care costs, including considering Medicare, Medicaid, long-term care insurance, and Health Savings Accounts (HSAs), is something you should definitely be doing. These tools and programs can help manage health care expenses in retirement, protecting your savings and ensuring that you receive the care you need.

Chapter 7

Brace Yourself - Estate Taxes Are Coming

"In this world, nothing is certain except death and taxes."
-**Benjamin Franklin, American Founding Father and inventor**

Understanding Estate & Inheritance Taxes

Anyone examining and planning for their financial legacy should have a decent knowledge of both these forms of taxation. While often lumped together, estate and inheritance taxes have different implications for how wealth is transferred after one's passing.

The Basics of Estate & Inheritance Taxes

At the heart of it, estate taxes are the dues paid on the value of what someone leaves behind. Think of it as a parting fee charged by the government before assets can be handed down, and it's the estate itself that's responsible for paying it. On the flipside, inheritance taxes are more personal. If you're lucky enough to inherit something, this tax is on what you receive, depending on where you live and what you're inheriting.

Regarding the big picture, the federal government focuses on estate taxes. They've set up a system in which only the hefty estates with values hitting a certain high-water mark need to worry about this tax. Think of this as a checkpoint that only the wealthier estates need to pass through, with the tax rate scaling up (from 18 to 40%) based on how much the estate is worth. It's a way of ensuring that when significant wealth is transferred from one generation to the next, a slice of it contributes back to the public, but only for those estates that are really up there in value (only over $13.61 million in 2024).

A Visionary's Blueprint: Steve Jobs & Estate Planning

Steve Jobs, the iconic co-founder of Apple, wasn't just a visionary in technology but also in managing his personal and financial affairs. Known for revolutionizing multiple industries—from personal computing and animated movies to music, smartphones, and tablet computing—Jobs' influence extended far beyond his company's innovative products. Despite his private battle with pancreatic cancer, Jobs meticulously planned for the future of his estate to ensure that his vast wealth, estimated at over $10 billion at the time of his passing in 2011, would be managed according to his wishes.

Steve Jobs's approach to estate planning reflected his foresight, with trusts established to benefit his family and minimize public scrutiny and estate taxes. This strategic planning included the establishment of the Steven P. Jobs Trust, which was later renamed the Laurene Powell Jobs Trust, indicating a well-thought-out plan for managing his assets posthumously. Jobs's legacy in estate planning showcases the importance of proactive measures, underscoring the value of trust and estate planning in safeguarding one's financial legacy, as well as supporting loved ones efficiently and discretely.

Who Pays Estate & Inheritance Taxes? How Are They Calculated?

Who's on the hook for taxes when someone passes away? For estate taxes, think of the estate itself as the one footing the bill. Before the assets are passed down, the estate is responsible for paying, but inheritance taxes are a bit different. If you're the one receiving the inheritance, you might be the one writing the check depending on where you live.

Calculating these taxes isn't as straightforward as you'd think. Estate taxes are all about the total value of what's left behind. The government sets a threshold, and the tax kicks in if the estate's value is above this limit. It's progressive, which means that there's a higher tax rate when the estate is worth more.

Let's paint a picture with some numbers. Imagine an estate valued at $3 million. Under current laws, if the exemption threshold is set at $13.61 million, this estate wouldn't owe any federal estate taxes. But flip the script to an estate worth, say, $15 million, and now a significant tax bill is calculated on the value over the threshold.

As for inheritance taxes, if you're inheriting in a state that levies this tax, the amount you pay can vary based on your relationship to the deceased and the value of what you inherit, making some gifts more costly than others.

Finding Exceptions and Exemptions: Tax-Free Thresholds

It's important to find your way around tax exceptions and exemptions. At the federal level, exemptions act as a sort of financial force field, shielding a portion of an estate's value from the grip of estate taxes. These exemptions are fairly generous and set a bar that many estates don't even reach, which means that a lot of families can pass on assets without worrying about a hefty tax bill from the federal government.

Let's simplify things: As of 2024, if your estate is worth less than $13.61 million, your estate won't owe any federal taxes. It's a significant boon, especially for those who are careful in their estate planning. This threshold acts as a protective bubble, ensuring that only the really large estates end up contributing a slice of their wealth to the public.

Note: Beginning in 2026, unless Congress acts to extend or change the law, the exemption amount is set to revert to pre-2018 levels, adjusted for inflation. This means that the exemption could potentially go back to around $5.5 - $6 million per individual, though the exact amount will depend on inflation rates.

This setup helps reduce estate tax burdens for many American families. By understanding and leveraging these exemptions, estate planners can strategically navigate the tax landscape, ensuring that the wealth accumulated over a lifetime is passed on according to their wishes, with as little as possible lost to taxes.

In the US, inheritance tax isn't as common—there are only six states that currently require it. And even then, it depends on the inheritance you receive. In Iowa, for example, if the estate is less than $25,000, no tax is due when it passes to the recipients. There are also further exemptions for heirs, so it depends on where you receive the inheritance and from whom.

Strategies for Minimizing Your Estate Tax Liability

Navigating the estate tax without stepping over any legal lines might sound like a high-wire act, but a few tried-and-true strategies can keep you grounded. The trick is to start early and think smart about how to lower what your estate could owe. Gifting is a classic move—it's a bit like handing out money before the government can claim its share. You can give away a certain amount each year to family members or friends tax-free, gradually reducing the size of your estate.

Then there's the trust, a favorite tool in the estate planner's kit. Setting up certain types of trusts can be like creating a legal fortress around parts of your estate, protecting it from hefty taxes. Trusts can be complex and tailored to specific assets or goals, but when done right, they're powerful in preserving more of your wealth. Both strategies, gifting and trusts, require navigating intricate rules and regulations.

Dodging Tax Bullets: Legal Ways to Reduce Estate Taxes

Gifting with a Purpose: Using Gifts to Lower Estate Taxes

Strategic gifting emerges as a savvy ally to ease the potential sting of estate taxes. By gifting assets during one's lifetime, the size of an estate will be smaller, leading to a lighter estate tax burden when the time comes.

The IRS provides a golden opportunity through the annual gift tax exclusion. This rule allows individuals to give away a certain amount of money or assets to as many people as they like each year, without these gifts counting toward the value of their estate or incurring gift tax. As of 2024, for instance, you could gift up to $18,000 per recipient annually without dipping into your lifetime estate and gift tax exemption or paying any gift tax. The lifetime gift limit is $13.61 million.

Note: In 2026, it's not just the estate tax exemption that may change. The gift tax exemption is also set to revert to its pre-2018 level, adjusted for inflation. This reversion, unless altered by new legislation, would reduce the exemption amount to around $5.5 - $6 million per individual.

This provision is a method to support loved ones, contribute to their financial stability, or even fund their educational pursuits, all while ensuring that your estate remains as tax-efficient as possible. Strategic use of the annual gift tax exclusion can significantly benefit both the giver and the receiver, turning gifting into a powerful tool in estate planning arsenals.

Trust the System: How Trusts Can Help Minimize Estate Taxes

Trusts offer a sophisticated way to manage assets and potentially reduce estate taxes. Among the various types, irrevocable trusts stand out for their tax efficiency. Unlike their revocable counterparts, which the grantor can alter or dissolve, irrevocable trusts are set in stone once established. This rigidity is precisely what makes them so valuable for estate tax planning.

You effectively remove assets from your estate when you transfer them to an irrevocable trust. These assets are no longer yours in the eyes of the law, and therefore they're not counted when calculating the value of your estate for tax purposes. This can lead to a significant reduction in estate taxes, as the assets in the trust may grow outside of your taxable estate. Additionally, irrevocable trusts can be designed to fulfill specific goals, such as providing for a loved one with special needs, protecting assets from creditors, or donating to charity.

The strategic use of trusts, especially irrevocable ones, requires careful planning and a clear understanding of the long-term implications. However, when executed correctly, they can offer a powerful means to preserve wealth for future generations while minimizing the impact of estate taxes.

Charitable Bequests: Giving Your Way to Lower Taxes

Charitable bequests help with tax efficiency, offering a meaningful way to leave a legacy while minimizing estate taxes. When you earmark a portion of your estate for charity, these donations can significantly lower the taxable value of your estate, thus reducing or even eliminating estate taxes altogether.

Consider the impact of a charitable bequest through this example: Let's say an estate valued at $15 million includes a $2 million donation to a charitable organization. This gesture not only honors the decedent's philanthropic spirit but also reduces the taxable estate to $13 million, potentially placing the estate below the threshold for federal estate taxes.

Moreover, estates that do owe taxes can benefit from charitable deduction provisions, in which the value of the bequest to a qualified charity is deductible from the gross estate. This can lead to substantial tax savings.

Strategically planning charitable bequests therefore furthers philanthropic goals *and* serves as an effective tool in estate planning.

A Vision Beyond the Horizon: Warren Buffett's Strategic Estate Planning

Warren Buffett, the renowned billionaire investor and philanthropist, provides a great example of strategic estate planning with a far-reaching vision. Known for his frugal lifestyle and immense wealth, Buffett has made headlines not just for his financial acumen but also for his commitment to giving away the majority of his fortune to charitable causes. He announced through a planned estate strategy that most of his wealth would be donated to the Bill and Melinda Gates Foundation and other charities upon his passing.

Buffett's approach to estate planning exemplifies how effective use of estate and inheritance tax laws can not only safeguard one's financial legacy but also channel vast resources toward making a significant impact on global issues. His decision to donate shares of his company, Berkshire Hathaway, instead of cash, further illustrates the thoughtful consideration of tax implications and asset management. Buffett's story is a powerful reminder of the potential of estate planning to extend one's influence and values far beyond one's lifetime, ensuring that wealth can continue to serve a purpose in line with one's deepest convictions.

Staying Current: SECURE Act & SECURE 2.0

The introduction of the SECURE Act and its sequel, SECURE 2.0[11], has reshaped the estate planning terrain significantly. These legislative updates have profound implications for how retirement assets are managed and passed on to heirs, directly impacting estate tax planning strategies.

A key takeaway from the SECURE Act is the elimination of the "stretch IRA" for most non-spouse beneficiaries, requiring inherited retirement accounts to be fully distributed within ten years. This accelerates the timeline for taxable distributions, potentially increasing the tax burden on heirs and affecting the estate's overall value.

SECURE 2.0 further adjusts this by offering new provisions that enhance retirement savings opportunities and planning flexibility. These include increased catch-up contributions for older savers and expanded options for tax-free withdrawals under certain conditions.

For those navigating estate planning, staying current on these changes is crucial. Adapting strategies to align with the new rules can help

---

[11] https://www.schwab.com/learn/story/inherited-ira-rules-secure-act-20-changes

maximize tax advantages, protect assets, and ensure that your financial legacy is passed on as efficiently as possible. Using a professional is likely your best course of action.

State-Specific Estate Tax Laws: What You Need to Know

How Does Your State Stack Up?

Estate and inheritance taxes vary widely from state to state, creating a patchwork of regulations that can significantly impact your estate planning strategy. While the federal government imposes its own estate tax, several states levy additional estate or inheritance taxes, each with its own set of rules and exemptions.

States like California and Florida stand out for their absence of state-level estate or inheritance taxes, making them potentially more attractive for those concerned about minimizing their tax burden. On the other hand, states such as New York and Maryland impose their own estate taxes with exemptions lower than the federal threshold, meaning that estates might be exempt from federal taxes but still owe state taxes.

Moreover, inheritance taxes, which are assessed on the beneficiaries rather than the estate itself, add another layer of complexity. Only a handful of states, including New Jersey and Pennsylvania, impose inheritance taxes, with the rate often depending on the beneficiary's relationship to the decedent. For instance, spouses are typically exempt, while distant relatives may face higher rates.

Because of all of these differences, it's clear that it's important to understand your state's specific laws. For example, an estate might face no state tax in Texas but could be subject to taxes if located in Oregon or Massachusetts, where estate tax rates and exemptions differ.

Crossing Borders: Dealing with Estate Taxes in Multiple States

When an estate spans multiple states, estate taxes can bring even more complexity. Each state's unique tax laws can introduce a maze of regulations, potentially complicating the estate planning process and increasing tax liabilities. This multi-state challenge requires a strategy to ensure a smooth passage for your estate's assets, minimizing the tax impact and safeguarding your legacy.

One strategy is establishing legal residency in one of those favorable tax law states. Residency dictates which state can levy taxes on your entire estate, not just the assets located within its borders. For those with homes in more than one state, choosing your state of residency wisely can lead to significant tax savings.

Additionally, consider using trusts to manage and distribute assets in different states. Certain types of trusts can offer protection against out-of-state estate taxes, allowing assets to bypass the probate process in multiple states.

Expert legal and financial planning is likely needed in these scenarios. Professionals with expertise in multi-state estate law can provide guidance tailored to your unique situation, helping with the complexities of state tax laws, domicile issues, and asset distribution.

Updates: Staying Current with Your State's Tax Law Changes

In estate planning, staying informed about changes in your state's tax laws is not only beneficial but also essential. Legislative shifts can dramatically alter the tax landscape, impacting strategies for minimizing your estate's tax liability. Keeping current with these changes ensures that your estate planning remains effective, adaptive, and aligned with current laws, safeguarding your assets from unforeseen tax burdens.

To navigate this, leverage various resources. State revenue department websites offer official updates and detailed explanations of tax laws, serving as a primary source of accurate information. Subscribing to newsletters from reputable tax and estate planning professionals can also provide insights into how new laws might affect your estate strategy.

Furthermore, attending seminars and workshops focused on estate planning and tax laws in your state can offer valuable opportunities to learn from experts and ask questions specific to your situation. For a more interactive approach, online forums and social media groups dedicated to estate planning also offer a platform.

Life Insurance for Estate Tax Planning

How Life Insurance May Benefit Your Estate Plan

Integrating life insurance into your estate plan can be a game changer, especially when it comes to providing liquidity and managing estate taxes efficiently. Life insurance proceeds can offer an influx of cash to your beneficiaries, ensuring that your estate has the necessary funds to cover taxes and other immediate financial obligations without hastily selling off assets.

One of the most compelling advantages of life insurance is its ability to bypass the probate process when beneficiaries are named directly on the policy. This means that the death benefit can be paid out quickly and directly to your loved ones. Moreover, these proceeds are generally income tax-free for the beneficiaries, providing a full-value financial benefit when they need it most.

Strategically, life insurance can also play a role in equalizing inheritances among beneficiaries. For instance, if the bulk of your estate is tied up in a business or real estate, life insurance can provide liquid assets to other heirs, ensuring that each beneficiary receives a fair share of your estate's value.

However, ensure that your beneficiary designations on your life insurance policies align carefully with your overall estate plan. Misalignments can lead to unintended consequences, potentially disrupting your intended asset distribution plan. Consulting with professionals can help you leverage life insurance effectively.

Death Benefits: How Are Life Insurance Proceeds Taxed?

Life insurance proceeds often provide crucial support in the aftermath of a loved one's passing. From a tax perspective, these proceeds typically arrive tax-free to beneficiaries. However, the tax-free nature of life insurance benefits is nuanced, and understanding the details is key to maximizing their utility within an estate plan.

While the direct receipt of life insurance proceeds by a beneficiary usually incurs no income tax, these funds can still influence the estate's overall value. It can potentially be subject to estate taxes if the insured's estate is named as the beneficiary or if the insured retains incidents of ownership in the policy. This distinction highlights the importance of careful beneficiary designation.

Irrevocable Life Insurance Trusts: A Tax-Reduction Strategy

Irrevocable life insurance trusts (ILITs) can be strategic to minimize estate taxes. By placing a life insurance policy in an ILIT, the proceeds are shielded from the taxable estate. This means that the life insurance payout doesn't add to the estate value subject to estate taxes upon the policyholder's death, allowing for a more efficient transfer of wealth to beneficiaries.

However, setting up an ILIT requires thoughtful consideration. First, the trust must be the policy owner from the start, or the policy must be transferred to it, in which case the transferor must survive the transfer by at least three years for it to be effective in removing the policy from their estate. Additionally, selecting the right trustee is crucial, as this individual will manage the trust and ensure that the policy premiums are paid and proceeds are distributed according to the grantor's wishes.

This maneuver requires foresight and careful planning, as it must be established well in advance of the policyholder's death to avoid inclusion in the estate for tax purposes, and so using a professional is advised.

Balancing Your Life Insurance with Your Estate Liquidity

Striking the right balance between your life insurance coverage and your estate's liquidity ensures that your estate can cover potential tax liabilities without burdening your heirs. Life insurance can infuse your estate with the liquidity needed to handle taxes, debts, and other obligations, protecting your assets from being sold under duress.

To gauge the appropriate level of coverage, evaluate your estate's estimated tax liabilities and liquidity needs upon your passing. This assessment should consider the size of your estate, anticipated tax rates, and any existing liquidity sources. Tailoring your life insurance coverage to address these factors can safeguard your estate's value and facilitate a smoother transition for your heirs.

Key Takeaways

1. **Estate vs. Inheritance Taxes:** Grasp the distinction between estate taxes (levied on the total value of the deceased's assets) and inheritance taxes (paid by the beneficiaries of those assets). Understanding who's responsible for these taxes can significantly influence your estate planning strategies.

2. **Tax-Free Thresholds and Exemptions:** Federal and state exemptions play a role in determining the taxable portion of an estate. Leveraging these exemptions through strategic planning can drastically reduce or even eliminate estate tax liabilities.

3. **Strategic Gifting:** Utilizing the annual gift tax exclusion reduces an estate's size, thereby lowering the potential estate tax burden. This

proactive approach benefits the giver and receiver, as well as strategically minimizes the overall estate tax impact.

4. **Trusts as a Tax Minimization Tool:** Incorporating trusts, especially irrevocable ones, into your estate plan can remove assets from your taxable estate. This offers a powerful method to shield wealth from hefty taxes while ensuring that your legacy is preserved according to your wishes.

5. **Charitable Bequests:** Donations made to charitable organizations from your estate can significantly reduce its taxable value, serving dual purposes of fulfilling philanthropic goals and achieving tax efficiency.

6. **Life Insurance Strategies:** Properly structured life insurance policies and trusts, like irrevocable life insurance trusts (ILITs), can provide the liquidity to cover general expenses or estate taxes.

Chapter 8

When Life Changes, Update Your Estate Plan

"The only thing you take with you when you're gone is what you leave behind."

-John Allston, motivational author and philosopher

Life Events That Should Trigger an Estate Plan Review

Milestones in your life aren't merely occasions for celebration but also a time for reevaluating your estate plan. Marriage, the birth of a child, divorce, and the loss of a loved one are events that can alter your financial and family obligations.

From "I Do" to "It's Over": How Marriage & Divorce Affect Your Estate Plan

Navigating life's big changes, like getting married or going through a divorce, greatly affects how you manage your estate plan. When you tie the knot, bringing your spouse into the fold of your financial and legal plans is fairly standard. You might find yourself updating[12] your estate

---

[12] https://www.kiplinger.com/retirement/estate-planning/603199/2021-estate-planning-checkup-is-your-estate-plan-up-to-date

plan to make sure that your partner is set up to manage things if you're not around, which often makes them the main beneficiary and possibly the executor of your will. It's all about ensuring the person you've built a life with is taken care of according to your plans together.

On the flipside, it'll be time to look at your estate plan again if things head toward divorce. This is when you'll want to sift through your beneficiary designations, like those for your life insurance and retirement accounts, to make sure that your ex isn't still the person set to inherit your assets. Don't forget to revise your will and any trusts you've set up, too. Leaving these as-is could mean that your assets end up somewhere you hadn't intended, which might not sit well with your current wishes or future plans.

Ignoring the need to update your estate plan after a divorce could lead to some unintended and maybe even messy outcomes, as some states will automatically cancel out any benefits to an ex-spouse in your will. Laws vary, and you don't want to leave things to chance.

New Arrival? Updating Your Estate Plan for Births and Adoptions

Welcoming a new family member, whether through birth or adoption, is a heartwarming milestone that calls for revisiting your estate plan. It's a prime time to ensure that your newest additions are properly accounted for and protected should anything unexpected happen. This means adjusting your will or trust to include them as beneficiaries, making sure that they're taken care of in the way you envision.

One of the steps in updating your estate plan with new children in mind is nominating a guardian. Should you and the other parent be unable to care for your child, a guardian will step in to make decisions on their behalf. It's a big decision involving a lot of trust, as this person or couple will guide your child through life in your absence.

Incorporating new children into your estate plan is also about ensuring that their upbringing and welfare align with your values and wishes and not simply about what they'll receive. It solidifies your intentions and provides a clear plan for their care and support.

A Beacon of Philanthropy: Chuck Feeney's "Giving While Living"

Chuck Feeney, co-founder of Duty Free Shoppers, was a master of estate planning through his "Giving While Living" philosophy. Amassing billions through his global retail empire, Feeney made the radical decision to donate most of his wealth to charitable causes during his lifetime. By transferring his fortune to the Atlantic Philanthropies, a collection of private foundations he created, Feeney set about anonymously funding education, science, healthcare, and civil rights projects worldwide.

His estate planning strategy was unique. Instead of bequeathing his wealth after his passing, Feeney utilized several trusts and legal mechanisms to dispense his assets while he could oversee and influence their impact. This approach allowed him to witness the fruits of his generosity and ensured that his philanthropic vision was executed precisely as he intended. Feeney's legacy challenges traditional notions of wealth accumulation and inheritance, demonstrating the profound impact and fulfillment that can result from a carefully planned and executed estate strategy focused on giving back.

When the Unthinkable Happens: Death, Disability, & Your Estate Plan

Life's unpredictability means that we sometimes face the unthinkable, like the death of a loved one named in our estate plan or confronting our potential incapacity. These moments compel us to look closely at our estate plans to ensure that they still serve our intended purpose. If a beneficiary or executor passes away, you'll need to update your estate plan to realign with your current situation and wishes.

Equally important is planning for one's own potential inability to make decisions for yourself down the road. Though it's hardly pleasant to think about, it's essential for a comprehensive estate plan. Establishing a durable power of attorney allows you to appoint someone you trust to manage your financial affairs if you're unable to do so. Similarly, a health care directive, also known as a living will, specifies your wishes regarding medical treatment and end-of-life care, and it names a health care proxy to make decisions on your behalf if you're incapacitated.

Taking these steps safeguards your assets and provides clear guidance to your loved ones during difficult times. It ensures that your wishes are honored, regardless of life's twists and turns, and helps avoid unnecessary stress and confusion for your family.

Regular Check-Ups: Why & When to Review Your Estate Plan

The Annual Review: What a Difference a Year Makes

An annual estate plan review is a wise idea for keeping your legacy aligned with your evolving life. Your estate plan likely requires yearly attention to ensure that it accurately reflects any financial and personal changes that have occurred. This process is about finetuning your plan to adapt to life's inevitable shifts like changes in asset values, family dynamics, or even your wishes themselves.

Asset valuation should be a focus during these reviews. The value of your investments, real estate, or business interests can fluctuate, impacting your estate's overall worth and how you might want to distribute assets. Similarly, updating beneficiary designations is smart practice. Life events such as marriages, births, and divorces can alter whom you want to benefit from your estate.

Trust provisions also need to be a focal point. The terms of any trusts you've established may need adjustments based on changes in tax laws, beneficiary needs, or your objectives. For instance, a trust set up for a child's education may require revisiting if that child decides not to pursue college.

An annual review ensures that your estate plan remains a true reflection of your current situation and goals. In short, it's a proactive approach to legacy planning.

Yes, Moving Impacts Your Estate Plan

Pulling up stakes and moving to a new state isn't just a logistical challenge—it can also impact your estate plan. The reason? As mentioned earlier, estate laws vary widely from state to state, which means the plan you put together in one jurisdiction might not work as intended in another. This can affect everything from the validity of your will to how your assets are taxed and distributed upon your passing.

For instance, some states honor community property rules that significantly affect asset division between spouses, while others stick to common law. This difference can reshape your estate distribution in ways you might not expect. Additionally, the state-specific nuances of probate law, estate tax thresholds, and even the formal requirements for a valid will (such as the number of witnesses) mean that you should double-check everything before moving.

An attorney versed in the estate laws of your new home state can help you navigate these changes, ensuring that your estate plan remains both compliant and optimized for your new circumstances. This might involve minor adjustments or a more comprehensive overhaul, but it needs to be done either way. Ensuring that your estate plan aligns with local laws means that you can rest easy.

Portfolio Check: Aligning Your Estate Plan with Your Financial Goals

It's best to examine your financial plan and investments to ensure that they align with your estate planning goals. Significant financial changes, such as a substantial increase or decrease in your investment portfolio's value, might mean reviewing your estate plan. These shifts could affect how you allocate assets among heirs or impact your plan's tax efficiency. For instance, a booming stock portfolio might elevate your estate's value to a point where it becomes liable for estate taxes, prompting the need for more strategic planning.

Moreover, major life events like receiving an inheritance, selling a business, or even retiring can significantly change your finances and, by extension, your estate planning needs. Such changes might lead to a reassessment of your beneficiaries, or perhaps integrating trusts into your plan to manage the newfound wealth.

Therefore, regular portfolio reviews not only keep your investment strategy on track but also ensure that your estate plan accurately reflects your current financial situation and goals. This proactive approach allows for a seamless transition of your legacy.

Safely Updating Your Will or Trust

More *Legalese*: Amendments, Codicils & Restatements

Tweaking your estate plan isn't as simple as penciling in new names or crossing out old ones on your will or trust documents. Instead, it involves formal legal procedures like amendments, codicils, or a complete restatement to ensure that your wishes are clear and legally enforceable. Understanding when and how to use each method is key to keeping your estate plan up to date.

An **amendment** applies to trusts and is essentially a modification to the existing document. It's used for smaller changes such as altering a beneficiary or trustee. However, if your trust has undergone several amendments, it might be time to consider a **restatement**. A restatement keeps the original trust in place but updates its contents, essentially replacing the old document with a new version that reflects all your changes over time.

For wills, the equivalent of an amendment is a **codicil**. This is a separate document that's attached to the will and details its changes. Codicils were more common when wills were typed or handwritten, but with today's digital availability, creating a new will might be simpler and clearer than attaching multiple codicils.

Deciding whether to amend, add a codicil, or restate depends on the extent of the changes you're making and the clarity you wish to maintain in your estate documents. Regardless of the method, formalizing changes through these legal processes ensures that your estate plan accurately reflects your current wishes and remains valid under the law.

DIY or Not: When to Involve a Lawyer in Your Estate Plan Changes

Deciding whether to DIY your estate plan updates or call in a professional boils down to the complexity of your changes and the intricacies of estate law. While minor adjustments might seem straightforward enough to handle independently, the devil is often in the details. For instance, simply adding a beneficiary might not be complex, but understanding the tax implications and ensuring that the change doesn't unintentionally affect other parts of your plan requires deeper knowledge of estate planning principles.

The risks of self-managed updates can be significant. Misinterpretations of legal requirements or overlooking the impact of changes can lead to disputes among heirs, unintended tax consequences, or even the invalidation of your documents.

Conversely, involving an estate planning lawyer ensures that every change is scrutinized for legal compliance with the rest of your estate plan. Lawyers can also foresee potential issues you might not have considered, from tax implications to future disputes, and offer solutions that align with your goals. The benefits of legal expertise are often worth the investment, especially with the complexities of estate law.

Signing Off: Properly Executing Your Updated Estate Plan

One of the fundamental requirements for executing updates to your estate documents, such as your will or trust, involves witness and notarization protocols. For instance, most states require that a will signed in the presence of two disinterested witnesses to be legally binding. These witnesses must not stand to benefit from the will and are often required to sign the document themselves, attesting to the testator's capacity and voluntary signing.

Notarization, while not always mandatory for wills, adds an additional layer of validity and is often required for other estate planning documents like powers of attorney and healthcare directives. A notary public verifies the signatories' identity, as well as understanding and willingness to sign the documents, providing an official seal that can help prevent disputes about the document's authenticity.

Lastly, if this wasn't clear previously, you should ensure secure storage of your updated estate planning documents. Keeping them in a safe, accessible place, and letting your executor or trustee know where to find them makes certain that your estate plan can be executed smoothly when the time comes. Some choose to store originals in a safety deposit box, with their attorney, or in a fireproof safe at home. Whichever method you choose, you need the right people to have access when needed without compromising the security of your sensitive information.

The Impact of Law Changes on Your Estate Plan

David Rockefeller's Legacy of Giving

Patriarch of the Rockefeller family and a towering figure in global banking, philanthropy, and art, David Rockefeller had crafted an estate plan that mirrored his lifelong commitment to philanthropy. He was known for his extensive art collection and generous charitable donations. Rockefeller ensured that his estate plan would continue his legacy of support for cultural, educational, and environmental causes long after his passing. By bequeathing significant assets, including valuable pieces of art to museums and substantial financial gifts to various charities, Rockefeller's estate plan is a testament to using wealth to foster societal progress and enlightenment.

Rockefeller's strategic approach to estate planning, which included creating trusts and making charitable bequests, exemplifies the potential of estate planning to extend one's impact on the world. His vision and actions highlight the role of thoughtful estate planning in achieving philanthropic goals, showcasing how structured giving can perpetuate a legacy of support for cherished causes and institutions.

How New Laws Affect Your Estate Plan

Legislative changes can significantly impact estate planning, potentially altering the effectiveness of your existing arrangements and the realization of your final intentions. Just as the ground shifts with the seasons, so too do the laws governing estate taxes, asset distributions, and fiduciary responsibilities. This means that you may need periodic reviews and to make adjustments to your estate plan to ensure that it remains updated with current legal standards and your personal wishes.

For instance, updates to federal estate tax laws might change the threshold for taxable estates, directly affecting your estate's tax liability and possibly requiring a strategy update to optimize tax benefits. Similarly, changes in state laws concerning powers of attorney, health care directives, or the recognition of digital assets could necessitate revisions to ensure that your estate plan is comprehensive and compliant.

Staying informed about these changes is the first step. Leverage the legal landscape to protect and preserve your legacy as efficiently as possible. This could mean subscribing to legal updates, working with an estate planning professional who stays current on legislative developments, or attending seminars and workshops on estate planning trends.

Understanding the dynamic nature of estate planning laws at both the federal and state levels, as well as adjusting your plan accordingly, ensures that your estate is prepared to navigate the legal complexities of tomorrow.

Examples of Tax Law Change Impact on Estate Plans

Recent shifts in tax laws can affect estate planning strategies. For instance, the Tax Cuts and Jobs Act of 2017 doubled the federal estate tax exemption, significantly altering estate planning strategies for many Americans. Before the change, an estate plan might have included complex strategies for minimizing estate taxes, but with the increased exemption, some families found themselves below the threshold.

Another example involves the Secure Act, enacted in December 2019, which changed the rules around inherited retirement accounts. Previously, beneficiaries could stretch distributions over their lifetimes, but now most must withdraw the funds within ten years, which affects income tax planning. This prompted many to reconsider named beneficiaries for IRAs and to explore alternatives, such as Roth conversions or life insurance policies.

Adapting to these changes requires a proactive approach, evaluating how new laws impact your situation and adjusting your estate plan accordingly.

Key Takeaways

1. **Life Events Necessitate Updates:** Major life milestones such as marriage, divorce, the birth or adoption of a child, and the death of a loved one significantly affect your estate plan, requiring timely updates.

2. **Annual Reviews are Essential:** Conducting an annual review of your estate plan ensures that it remains aligned with your financial situation, personal relationships, and any changes in the law.

3. **State Laws Impact Estate Plans:** Relocating to a different state can have implications for your estate plan due to variations in state laws regarding estate taxes, asset distribution, and legal document requirements.

4. **Formal Updates for Legal Documents:** Modifying your estate plan through amendments, codicils, or restatements must be done with formal legal procedures to ensure that changes are legally valid and enforceable.

5. **Professional Guidance is Key:** The complexities of tax law changes and the intricacies of estate planning underscore the importance of seeking professional advice. Estate planning

professionals can deal with legal nuances, ensuring that your plan is compliant and strategically aligned with your goals.

6. **Stay Informed on Law Changes:** Knowledge of tax and estate law changes is great for proactive estate planning. Leveraging professional advisories, attending educational events, and consulting with estate planning professionals can help you adapt your plan to current laws.

Chapter 9

Probate Keeping Calm and Carrying On

> "I found that when you have to teach something, you get to know it better yourself."
> -John Grisham, bestselling author and former attorney

How Does Probate Work? A Closer Look

We've mentioned probate often throughout this book thus far, but let's further examine this concept and what it involves. Probate[13] often appears to be a complicated process filled with legal jargon and procedures, but it's often unavoidable and serves as the judicial method to oversee the distribution of a deceased person's estate. This chapter will peel back the complexity surrounding probate, outlining what it entails, how it operates, and why understanding this process is necessary for effective estate planning.

The Probate Process: From Death to Division

In simple terms, probate is the legal process that kicks in after someone passes away, from proving that the will is real to ensuring that assets end up in the right hands. It starts with filing the will in probate court. This is where the court determines if the will is valid and reflects the deceased person's final wishes according to state laws.

---

[13] https://www.investopedia.com/terms/p/probate.asp

Next, the court appoints an executor. This is usually someone who the deceased named in the will, tasked with the big job of managing the estate through probate. Their to-do list includes gathering all the deceased's assets, which means that everything they owned has to be listed and valued. It's a bit like taking inventory of a person's life in financial terms.

After determining what the estate is worth, the executor uses the estate's funds to pay off any debts and taxes owed. Only after these bills are settled can they move on to the final step: handing out what's left to the people named in the will or, if there's no will, according to the state's rules on inheritance. This last part is where the assets finally make their way to the new owners, wrapping up the probate process from death to the division of assets.

Knowing Your Probate Lingo

Getting familiar with the relevant probate terminology is a bit like learning a new language, but it's important in ensuring that the probate process goes smoothly. Although these key terms have been touched upon already, it's important that they're fully understood, **so here's another quick rundown:**

- **Executor:** This is the person named in the will who's in charge of the estate. Think of them as the estate's project manager, handling everything from paperwork to paying bills and distributing assets.

- **Beneficiary:** Anyone named in the will who's set to receive something, whether it's a family heirloom or a chunk of cash, is a beneficiary. They're essentially on the receiving end of the estate's distribution.

- **Intestate:** If someone dies without a will, they've died intestate. In this case, state laws step in to decide who gets what, which can lead to some unexpected outcomes if the deceased never made their wishes known.

- **Testamentary Trust:** This is set up within a will and kicks into action after death. It's a way to put conditions on an inheritance, like holding assets until a beneficiary reaches a certain age.

Executors and Administrators: Who They Are & What They Do

These are the quarterbacks of probate, leading the estate through the legal process after someone passes away. An executor is someone who's named to manage the deceased's estate, and the court appoints an administrator if there's no will (or if the named executor can't take on the role). Either way, their job is to carry out the deceased's wishes and settle the estate.

Their to-do list is pretty comprehensive. It includes filing the will with the probate court, gathering and valuing the deceased's assets, paying off debts and taxes, and distributing what's left to the rightful heirs. They're also on the hook for keeping detailed records and communicating with beneficiaries about how and when the assets will be distributed.

You'll want the right person for this job. It needs to be someone you trust to manage your affairs with integrity, but they must also be organized and ready to ensure a complex legal process. It's about ensuring that your estate is handled smoothly and your beneficiaries are cared for without unnecessary stress or conflict.

Will or No Will: Probate Considerations

Whether you leave behind a will or not makes a big difference in how your estate works after you're gone. With a will, you've left a roadmap that guides the probate court on who gets what, making the process more straightforward.

Conversely, dying without a will (or dying intestate, as mentioned above) leaves the fate of your estate in the hands of state laws. These laws dictate a default inheritance plan, which might not match your chosen choice. The court will appoint an administrator to handle your estate and your assets will be distributed according to a predetermined formula, typically favoring spouses and blood relatives. This process can be lengthier and more complicated, possibly leading to results you wouldn't have intended.

Preserving Artistic Legacy: Pablo Picasso's Estate Challenges

Pablo Picasso left behind a vast and valuable estate at the time of his death in 1973, including thousands of his artworks. However, Picasso passed away without a will, leading to prolonged legal battles among his heirs. The reason? He was superstitious, but the complications that followed were likely not worth Picasso's unfounded fears. This situation exemplifies the complexities and potential pitfalls of not having a clear estate plan, especially for those with significant and unique assets

Avoiding Probate[14]: How Smart Estate Planners Do It

A Legacy of Innovation: George Lucas' Philanthropic Strategy

The visionary filmmaker behind "Star Wars," George Lucas orchestrated a forward-thinking estate plan emphasizing philanthropy. After selling his TV and film production company Lucasfilm to Disney

---

[14] https://www.forbes.com/advisor/legal/estate-law/how-avoid-probate/

in 2012, Lucas pledged most of the proceeds to education initiatives. This move highlights the strategic use of estate planning to support lifelong passions and commitments beyond one's lifetime. Lucas' approach emphasizes the potential of estate planning to channel personal success into societal benefits, making a lasting impact on future generations. It certainly doesn't need to be in a galaxy far, far away.

Durable Power of Attorney: A Strong Probate Bypass

A durable power of attorney (DPOA) is essentially giving the keys to your finances to a friend who can manage your affairs if you can't. A regular power of attorney becomes invalid if you're incapacitated, but a DPOA stays in effect, providing a way to handle your finances without court intervention. This tool can be extremely useful, especially when trying to bypass probate for certain aspects of your estate.

With a DPOA, you appoint someone you trust to make financial decisions for you. This can include paying your bills, helping you with your investments, or even selling property. Because this person can act for you, assets managed under a DPOA often don't need to go through probate. This means quicker access to funds for paying expenses and less red tape for your loved ones.

However, there's a catch: You need to have this document in place before it's required. If you become unable to manage your affairs without a DPOA determined, your family might have to go through a lengthy and potentially stressful court process to obtain permission to act on your behalf. Setting up a DPOA is a proactive step that ensures that your financial matters are handled smoothly, keeping your estate's management in trusted hands.

Living Trusts: Your Secret Weapon Against Probate

Stealthy in estate planning, living trusts help your assets slip past the probate process unnoticed. Essentially, a living trust is a legal document that places your assets into a trust during your lifetime, and then transfers the assets to the beneficiaries when you pass away. The key advantage? Assets in a living trust don't go through probate.

Setting up a living trust involves drafting a trust document, which is like a blueprint that outlines how your assets should be managed and eventually distributed. You'll need to name a trustee who can manage the trust's assets. This can be yourself initially, with a successor trustee stepping in after your passing.

The next step is to fund the trust by transferring assets into it. This could be anything from bank accounts to your apartment rentals. It's a necessary step because only the assets in the trust will bypass probate. While setting up a living trust might seem like a lot of upfront work, the payoff is significant.

Joint Ownership: Another Way to Avoid Probate

Two or more people owning property together is referred to as joint ownership, which acts as a straightforward passageway for assets to transfer directly to the surviving owner(s) upon one's death. This mechanism is particularly effective with real estate, bank accounts, and vehicles. The two main types of joint ownership facilitating this transfer are joint tenancy with right of survivorship, and tenancy by the entirety (which is specifically for married couples in some states).

However, while joint ownership can simplify the transfer of assets and ensure that they remain accessible to the surviving owner, it's not without its complications. For one, it involves giving up a degree of control over the asset since all owners must agree on any decisions regarding the property. Additionally, the asset becomes vulnerable to the creditors that any of the owners might have; if one owner faces legal action or bankruptcy, the asset could be at risk.

One more thing to note is the potential for effects to your estate planning. Adding a joint owner essentially means that you're giving away part of the asset during your lifetime, which might not align with your overall estate plan or intentions for asset distribution after your death. Thus, while joint ownership offers a probate bypass, you should weigh its benefits against these considerations and potential pitfalls.

POD & TOD Accounts: Often-Underutilized Tools

Payable on death (POD) and transfer on death (TOD) accounts are often used in estate planning, as they allow assets to glide smoothly to beneficiaries without getting caught in probate. POD accounts are typically used for bank accounts, whereas TOD arrangements can apply to securities and even real estate in some jurisdictions.

Here's how they work: You designate a beneficiary (or beneficiaries) to receive the assets in the account after you pass away. The beauty of POD and TOD accounts lies in their simplicity. The assets don't need to pass through probate, as the accounts are designed to transfer directly to the named beneficiaries who merely need to provide identification and a death certificate to claim their inheritance.

The advantages? Speed and simplicity. These accounts allow for a quick transfer of assets, helping beneficiaries avoid the lengthy and potentially costly probate process. Additionally, they offer flexibility. You can change beneficiaries without much hassle and the designations are revocable, meaning that you can adjust your plans as life circumstances change.

However, use these tools wisely and ensure that they fit within your broader estate planning strategy. POD and TOD designations can be powerful, but they must align with your overall intentions for asset distribution to avoid unintended consequences or disputes among heirs.

Navigating Probate: A Step-by-Step Guide

Getting the Probate Process Started

The first task with probate is obtaining the death certificates, since you'll need these for just about everything moving forward—from closing accounts to initiating the probate process. Next, you'll need to locate the deceased's will, assuming there is one.

Once you have the death certificate and the will in hand, the next move is to file a petition with the probate court to start the process officially. This usually involves submitting the will, the death certificate, and a petition form that details the deceased, their family, their assets, and the named executor.

Timeliness and organization are your best friends in this regard. Starting the probate process promptly ensures that the estate is settled as smoothly and quickly as possible, minimizing the chances for complications or disputes.

What's It All Worth? Appraising the Estate's Value

Figuring out what an estate is truly worth is a challenging part of the probate process. This step involves appraising the estate's assets, from bank accounts and stocks to real estate and personal belongings.

The appraisal process is meticulous. It often requires professionals who can accurately value many assets and ensure that everything is accounted for at its current market value. This valuation sets the stage for everything that follows in probate, including paying off debts and taxes and eventually distributing assets to heirs.

Why is getting this right so important? An accurate valuation ensures fairness and potentially more transparency in the probate process. It helps prevent disputes among beneficiaries by providing a clear basis for asset distribution. Moreover, it's essential for settling the estate's debts and obligations without shortchanging creditors or taxing authorities. If the estate is undervalued, there might not be enough to cover debts, and if overvalued, beneficiaries might face unnecessary taxes.

A Clean Slate: Paying Debts, Taxes & Liabilities

Once the estate's assets have been appraised, the next phase in probate is clearing the slate of any financial obligations. This involves paying off the estate's debts, taxes, and any other liabilities. The executor must first identify all outstanding debts including personal loans, credit card bills, and mortgages. They're also responsible for settling any final income taxes for the deceased and the estate.

There's a proper sequence in which these payments are made. Generally, there's a legal order to follow, prioritizing certain debts over others. For instance, funeral and last-illness expenses often top the list, followed by taxes and general creditors. This pecking order is crucial because it ensures that the estate is settled properly and in line with the law.

The Finish Line: Distributing the Remaining Assets

Crossing this crucial endpoint in the probate process means getting to the part where the balance of the assets are finally distributed as outlined in the will (or according to state laws if there isn't one). This step is the culmination of all the careful planning, valuation, and settling of debts, in which the executor's role shifts from manager and mediator to distributor.

Before distribution can happen, the executor needs to ensure that all debts, taxes, and liabilities have been paid off. Once that's cleared, they can start the process of transferring the assets. This might involve signing over deeds, transferring titles of vehicles, or simply writing checks from the estate's account.

The final duty of the executor is to close the estate. This involves providing the probate court with a detailed account of everything that's been done—assets collected, debts paid, and distributions made. The executor can officially close the estate once the court approves this final accounting.

The Nasty Realities of Disputes During Probate

When Heirs Clash: Understanding Probate Disputes

Probate disputes among heirs can turn the process of settling an estate from a straightforward legal procedure into a complex, emotional battleground. Common causes of such disputes include disagreements over the interpretation of the will, perceived inequalities in asset distribution, or challenges to the validity of the will itself, perhaps due to concerns about undue influence or the mental capacity of the deceased when the will was made.

Another frequent source of conflict arises when one heir believes that the executor isn't performing their duties fairly or efficiently, leading to mistrust and contention among family members. Additionally, blended families often face unique challenges as step-relatives and children from different marriages vie for their share of the estate.

Transparency and communication throughout the probate process can help preempt and manage these tensions. This includes having detailed discussions about the will and estate plan before death, which can help set clear expectations and reduce surprises that could lead to disputes. Utilizing mediation services to resolve conflicts when they arise can also preserve family relationships by avoiding the adversarial nature of court proceedings.

Ultimately, the goal in managing probate disputes is to honor the wishes of the deceased while ensuring fair treatment of all heirs.

Contesting a Will: When, Why & How

Heirs or beneficiaries can initiate this legal challenge if they believe that the will doesn't accurately reflect the deceased's intentions due to various factors. Common grounds for contesting a will include undue influence (whereby an argument is made that the deceased was pressured into making decisions), lack of testamentary capacity (the deceased wasn't mentally capable of understanding the will's implications), fraudulent wills, or if the will wasn't executed correctly according to state laws (improper witnessing or lack of a signature).

Contesting a will begins with filing a petition in probate court. Usually, this must be done within a specific time frame, which varies by state, after the will has been filed for probate. The contesting party must then provide evidence to support their claim. This often involves legal representation, witness testimony, and, sometimes, medical records.

The impact of contesting a will can be significant, potentially halting the probate process until the dispute is resolved. This can delay the distribution of assets, incur additional legal fees, and strain familial relationships. Moreover, if the contest is successful, the court may invalidate the entire will or specific provisions, leading to assets being distributed under state intestacy laws or according to a previous will, altering the deceased's intended asset distribution.

Resolving Conflicts Outside the Court with Mediation

Mediation offers a less adversarial route for resolving probate disputes, focusing on collaboration and communication to find a mutually acceptable solution. This process involves a neutral third party, the mediator, who facilitates discussions between the disputing parties, helping them explore options for settlement that might not be available in a court setting. The mediator doesn't make decisions like a judge does, but simply guides the parties toward their own resolution.

The major benefit of mediation is the preservation of family relationships. Probate disputes can be emotionally charged, and litigation often exacerbates tensions, leading to lasting rifts. Mediation, by contrast, encourages open dialogue and understanding, fostering a cooperative environment where all voices are heard and considered. This can be especially important in maintaining family bonds after the resolution.

Additionally, mediation can preserve the estate's value by avoiding the high costs associated with court proceedings. Legal fees can be expensive and may use significant estate assets. By resolving disputes through mediation, parties can significantly reduce these costs, ensuring that more of the estate goes to the heirs as intended.

Moreover, mediation offers a level of privacy and control not available in court. The process is confidential, keeping sensitive family matters out of the public eye. Parties also have more control over the outcome, crafting an agreement that works for everyone involved rather than having a resolution imposed by a judge.

The Role of the Probate Court in Resolving Disputes

The probate court can help mediate conflicts arising during the probate process, acting as the final say when parties cannot agree. Its primary function is to ensure that the deceased's estate is distributed according to the will's provisions—or in the absence of a will, according to state intestacy laws—while safeguarding all involved parties' rights.

When a dispute is brought before the probate court, it follows a structured legal procedure. This usually begins with a formal filing that outlines the nature of the dispute, whether it's contesting the will's validity, disagreements over the interpretation of the will's terms, or conflicts regarding the executor's actions. The court then schedules hearings in which all parties can bring their evidence and talk through their arguments.

The probate court's intervention is characterized by its commitment to a fair and lawful resolution. Judges consider all presented evidence and apply laws for the final outcome.

Moreover, the probate court also provides a structured environment for resolving disputes, which can help prevent the escalation of family tensions and ensure that the estate settlement process proceeds orderly.

Key Takeaways

1. **Understanding Probate:** Knowing the probate process, from initiation to asset distribution, is necessary to effectively manage an estate.

2. **The Importance of a Will:** Having a will simplifies the probate process by clearly outlining the deceased's wishes for asset distribution, making it easier for the executor to fulfill their duties and for beneficiaries to receive their inheritance.

3. **Strategies to Bypass Probate:** Tools such as durable power of attorney, living trusts, joint ownership, and POD/TOD accounts can reduce the estate's exposure to probate.

4. **The Value of Timely and Organized Action:** Initiating the probate process promptly and maintaining organized records are key to a smooth estate settlement, minimizing potential disputes and delays.

5. **Mediation as a Conflict Resolution Tool:** Mediation can be an effective method for resolving probate disputes outside of court, as well as preserving family relationships, estate value, and privacy. It offers a more cost-effective and collaborative approach to dispute resolution.

6. **The Probate Court's Role in Dispute Resolution:** When disputes cannot be resolved through mediation, the probate court ensures a fair and lawful resolution based on the will's terms or state intestacy laws, safeguarding the interests of all parties involved. This underscores the court's importance in upholding the probate process's integrity and ensuring that the deceased's wishes are honored.

Chapter 10

Seize the Day Taking Control of Your Estate Plan Now

Overcoming Procrastination: Why There's No Time Like the Present

In estate planning, procrastination[15] is a common adversary that many of us face, often leaving decisions for "another day." But the reality is that the right time to address our estate planning needs is now—not in the future.

The Perils of Procrastination: Unveiling the Risks of Delaying Estate Planning

Waiting too long to sort your estate plan is playing with your family's needs. Without a will or a solid plan, you're basically letting state laws call the shots on who gets what. This could mean that your hard-earned assets might not end up with the people you wanted them to go to, and no one wants that situation.

---

[15] https://michaelbaileylawllc.com/just-get-started-overcoming-procrastination-and-fear-in-setting-up-your-estate-plan/

Next, there's the convoluted matter of probate. Not having a will means a longer, more complicated process for your loved ones to endure, which can consume both time and money that could've been better spent elsewhere. Also, without clear directions from you, family squabbles over who gets what can quickly escalate, turning what should be a time of coming together into a nightmare. Getting your estate planning in order sooner rather than later isn't just smart—it's also a measure for keeping the peace and making sure that your wishes are carried out properly.

Motivational Tips to Kickstart Your Estate Planning

Beginning the estate planning process doesn't have to be arduous or fearsome. First, jot down some clear goals. What do you want to achieve with your state plan? Who do you want to protect? Getting these ideas out of your head and onto paper can make the process feel more tangible and less like a chore.

Next, condense everything that needs to be done into bite-sized pieces. Start with something straightforward, like listing out your assets or considering who you'd trust as an executor. Small steps lead to progress in time.

Also, never be embarrassed to ask for direction. Estate planning professionals can help translate all the *legalese* into plain English and help you through the process, ensuring that you don't miss anything. You need to just grab a pen, make the call, and start plotting your course.

Safe and Sound: Strong Practices for Storing Your Estate Planning Documents

There are many places where you can secure your estate planning documents, with a few highlighted below:

- **Safety Deposit Box:** This option offers high security, but it can be hard to access quickly, so ensure that someone else knows about it and can access it if needed.

- **Secure but Accessible Location in Home:** You can use a secure place in your dwelling, but be sure to use a fireproof and waterproof safe that's accessible to you and trusted individuals without making it too easy for others to find.

- **Store with Your Attorney:** Storing your documents with your lawyer has many benefits. It keeps documents well-guarded and adds professional oversight, and your attorney can act promptly when necessary.

- **Digital Copies:** This is a wise option for backing up your documents. Make sure to use encrypted storage or secure cloud services, but remember that they don't actually replace the originals.

- **Inform Trusted Individuals:** Make sure that at least one trusted person knows where your documents are and how to access them, which reduces delays in the case of emergencies.

- **Regular Reviews and Updates:** Life changes mean that estate plans need to evolve, so review documents annually or after any major life events.

- **Keep an Inventory:** A detailed list of document locations helps executors and family members quickly find what they need, streamlining the process.

From Deeds to Passwords: A Comprehensive List of What You Need

There are many things you need to keep together with your estate plan. Below, a list of things to keep in mind:

- **Last Will and Testament:** This is the biggest one for any estate plan. The last will and testament outlines who inherits your assets and, if applicable, guardianship wishes for minor children.

- **Revocable Living Trust:** This measure will help your estate bypass the lengthy and public probate process, providing a seamless transition of assets to your beneficiaries.

- **Beneficiary Designations:** These can override information in wills and trusts for specific accounts or joint assets.

- **Advance Healthcare Directive/Living Will:** These documents communicate your healthcare preferences in scenarios during which you can't make decisions yourself, including end-of-life care.

- **Property Deeds and Titles:** Essential records proving ownership of your property and vehicles, these are important for smooth transfer upon your passing.

- **Digital Logins and Passwords:** As digital assets become more prevalent, ensuring access to these for executors or trusted individuals is increasingly important.

- **List of Your Assets:** A detailed inventory of all your assets is helpful in the management of your estate, especially if it has to enter the probate process.

- **Identification of Your Debts:** A clear record of debts ensures that your executor can settle outstanding balances, preventing unexpected claims against your estate.

Peace of Mind with Your Estate Plan: Breathing Easy

The Comfort of Knowing Your Wishes Will Be Honored

A deep sense of relief and peace comes from having a comprehensive estate plan in place. It's about knowing that your wishes for your assets, healthcare, and legacy will be respected and followed. This assurance can significantly ease your mind and reduce stress, not just for you but for your loved ones, who'll find comfort in understanding your desires and knowing how to honor them.

Environmental Legacy: Ted Turner's Conservation Efforts

Media mogul and philanthropist Ted Turner has long been an advocate for environmental conservation and sustainable practices. Beyond his lifetime, Turner's commitment to the planet is secured through his estate planning, which includes significant contributions to land conservation and environmental initiatives.

Turner's establishment of the Turner Foundation is a huge part of his estate planning, focusing on environmental conservation and showcasing how estate planning can extend one's passion and advocacy for causes into the future. This strategic approach ensures that his wealth supports the preservation of natural habitats and promotes sustainable environmental practices for generations to come.

Financial Security

A well-crafted estate plan helps with financial security for your beneficiaries. It ensures that your assets are distributed according to your wishes and provide for your family's needs, education, or any specific financial support you wish to leave behind. By clearly outlining your financial wishes, you can protect your loved ones from the unpredictability of probate and ensure that they have the means to maintain or improve their quality of life.

Tax Efficiency

An estate plan built with tax efficiency in mind can save your beneficiaries significant taxes. Through careful planning and strategies such as trusts, charitable contributions, and the timely distribution of assets, you can minimize the tax liabilities that your estate and heirs may face. This approach maximizes the inheritance that your beneficiaries will receive.

Control Over Your Legacy

Estate planning isn't about simply disbursing your assets—it's a way to leave a lasting impression on the world and shape how you're remembered. Whether it's through charitable giving, passing down heirlooms, or even the values instilled in your will, a thoughtful estate plan allows you to control your legacy. It's your final opportunity to reflect your life's values, accomplishments, and the mark you wish to leave on your loved ones and the community.

Crafting a Legacy: Leona Helmsley's Charitable Trust

Leona Helmsley, the "Queen of Mean," was known for her real estate empire and infamous personality, and yet her estate planning revealed a different aspect of her legacy. Helmsley left a substantial portion of her wealth to the Leona M. and Harry B. Helmsley Charitable Trust, directing billions toward various philanthropic causes.

This move showcased the power of estate planning to support charitable endeavors on a grand scale, impacting health care, education, and urban community improvement long after her passing. Helmsley's estate plan highlights how even the most controversial figures can leave a positive mark on the world through thoughtful preparation and clear directives.

Being Prepared for the Unknown

Life is full of uncertainties, but a comprehensive estate plan provides stability amidst the unknown. It prepares you and your loved ones for unforeseen events, whether they're financial, health related, or even legal challenges. Estate planning empowers you to face the future with confidence, secure in the knowledge that your affairs are in order and your family is protected, no matter what life (and death) throws your way.

Key Takeaways

1. **Procrastination is a Barrier to Peace of Mind:** Delaying estate planning can lead to unnecessary complications, stress for your

loved ones, and the risk of your wishes not being honored. Taking action now ensures that your intentions are clear and legally documented.

2. **Estate Planning Provides Emotional and Financial Security:** Knowing that your estate plan is in place offers comfort and assures your beneficiaries of their financial future, reducing anxiety and potential conflicts after you're gone.

3. **Tax Efficiency Maximizes Your Legacy:** Strategic estate planning can significantly reduce tax liabilities, ensuring that more of your assets are passed on to your beneficiaries rather than to tax obligations.

4. **Maintaining Control Over Your Legacy:** A comprehensive estate plan allows you to dictate the distribution of your assets, the care of your dependents, and the continuation of your values.

5. **Preparation for Life's Uncertainties:** Estate planning is crucial in preparing for the unpredictable, safeguarding your estate and your loved ones' well-being against unforeseen challenges while ensuring that your wishes are followed.

6. **Best Practices for Document Storage Are Essential:** Properly storing and managing your estate planning documents—making them accessible yet secure and keeping them updated—protects against loss, damage, or delays in carrying out your wishes.

Closing Remarks

Throughout this guide, we've embarked on a comprehensive journey, navigating the essentials of estate and retirement planning and delving into the complexities of wills, trusts, and tax strategies. This exploration has illuminated the path to securing financial stability and protecting loved ones, and it's also empowered you with the knowledge to make informed decisions. By addressing these critical topics head-on, we've clarified the processes involved in estate planning and provided you with the tools needed for proactive planning.

The empowerment gained through this knowledge offers more than just practical benefits—it provides a profound peace of mind knowing that your future and the well-being of your loved ones are well-guarded. This book guides you to take control of your estate planning with confidence and foresight.

Recap of Major Themes

At the heart of this book lies the importance of organizing assets, safeguarding the future of loved ones, and cementing a lasting legacy through thoughtful estate planning. The process simplifies the complexities of asset distribution and ensures that no valuable piece of your financial life is overlooked or lost in transition.

Examining the legal frameworks of wills, trusts, and advance directives has shown you the tools and mechanisms you have at your disposal to navigate the often intricate process of estate planning. Understanding these instruments is an important step—each serves a unique purpose in protecting assets, minimizing taxes, and fulfilling your final wishes.

This guide has stressed the indispensable role of these legal structures in avoiding probate, ensuring that healthcare wishes are respected, and providing for loved ones after your passing.

Furthermore, this book has intricately woven together the concepts of retirement and estate planning, highlighting how they're connected. Early and thoughtful preparation in these areas isn't just about securing financial stability—it's also about creating a future that aligns with personal values and wishes.

Key Takeaways of the Book

The main takeaway is that you need to take control of your financial and personal future through proactive planning. There's an emphasis on the understanding that the nuances of estate laws and retirement provisions are both beneficial and essential. Regular updates to your estate plan in response to life's inevitable changes and legal shifts ensure that your wishes remain aligned with your current situation. They also safeguard your legacy and the well-being of your loved ones.

Moreover, we've emphasized that professional consultation can be extremely helpful. Navigating estate and retirement planning is complex, and this is where the expertise of financial advisors, estate lawyers, and tax professionals can provide clarity, peace of mind, and strategic direction. This book serves as a comprehensive resource, equipping you with the tools and knowledge to confidently begin. It's a call to action, a reminder that the best time to plan for the future is now. It ensures that when life's next chapter begins, it unfolds how you want it to.

Now is the time to take your first step toward estate planning—you're equipped with the insights and strategies in this book to ensure that you're well on your way. Don't hesitate to implement your newfound knowledge and begin shaping a future that reflects your desires and needs.

Share how this guide has influenced your estate planning process and the positive changes it's brought to your life by leaving a review on Amazon or another relevant platform. Remember—estate planning is an ongoing journey that requires continual learning and adaptation to accommodate your life, and helping others find it will put everyone in a better place.

With this book, you've taken an enormous step toward securing a financially stable and deeply fulfilling future. With the guidance provided here, as well as a commitment to thoughtful planning, you're well-positioned to navigate the path ahead. Rest assured that with the right plans in place, you can look forward to a rewarding retirement and the peace of mind that comes from knowing that your legacy will endure.

Estate Planning A to Z Glossary

Annual Exclusion: The amount of money that one person may give to another within one year without incurring a gift tax or affecting the unified credit.

Asset: Any resource owned or controlled by an individual or business entity.

Basis: For property held by one's self, it's the purchase price plus costs and improvements minus depreciation taken. For inherited property, it's usually the fair market value of the property at the time of the decedent's death, regardless of what the decedent paid for the property.

Beneficiary: An individual or entity that receives benefits, profits, or advantages from something—particularly a trust, will, or life-insurance policy.

Charitable Remainder Trust: A tax-exempt irrevocable trust designed to reduce the taxable income of individuals. It does this by dispersing income to the beneficiaries of the trust for a specified period of time and then donating the remainder of the trust to the designated charity.

Codicil: An addition or supplement that explains, modifies, or revokes a will (or part of one).

Community Property: A type of joint ownership of assets between married couples, commonly recognized in several US states.

Conservator: A person, official, or institution designated to take over and protect the interests of an incompetent.

Decedent: The person who has died.

Digital Assets: Any information or data that exists in digital form and comes with the right to use. This can include photographs, emails, social media accounts, and cryptocurrencies.

Estate Planning: The preparation of tasks that serve to manage an individual's asset base in the event of their incapacitation or death.

Estate Tax: A tax on the transfer of a deceased person's estate.

Executor: An individual or institution appointed by a testator to carry out the terms of their will.

Gift Tax: A federal tax applied to an individual giving anything of value to another person.

Grantor: The individual who creates a trust and contributes property to it.

Gross Estate: The total property held by an individual as defined for federal estate tax purposes.

Guardian: An individual who is legally responsible for the care of someone unable to manage their own affairs, especially a minor or disabled person.

Heir: A person legally entitled to the property or rank of another upon that person's death.

Inheritance Tax: A tax paid by a person who inherits money or property, or a levy on the estate of a person who has died.

Intestate: Dying without a will.

Irrevocable Trust: A trust that can't be modified or terminated without the permission of the beneficiary.

Joint Tenancy: A legal arrangement in which two or more people own a property together, each with equal rights and obligations.

Living Trust: A legal document created by an individual, known as the grantor, during their lifetime. The trust holds ownership of the grantor's assets.

Marital Deduction: A deduction allowing for the unlimited transfer of any or all property from one spouse to the other, generally free of estate and gift tax.

Pour Over Will: A legal document ensuring that an individual's remaining assets will automatically transfer to a previously established trust upon their death.

Power of Attorney: A legal document giving one person (the agent or attorney-in-fact) the power to act for another person (the principal).

Probate: The legal process through which a deceased person's estate is properly distributed to heirs and designated beneficiaries, and through which any debt owed to creditors is paid off.

Qualified Terminable Interest Property (QTIP): Property that transfers from decedent to surviving spouse, qualifying for marital deduction and thus avoiding estate tax until the death of the surviving spouse.

Retained Interest: In a trust, a right to receive benefit from the property that isn't given away, resulting in reduced gift tax.

Revocable Trust: A trust in which provisions can be altered or canceled dependent on the grantor.

Step-Up in Basis: The readjustment of the value of an appreciated asset for tax purposes upon inheritance.

Tangible Personal Property Memorandum (TPPM): A legal document that's referred to in a will. It lists and describes personal property and gives specific instructions for the distribution of the property.

Tenancy in Common: A type of ownership in which two or more people have an undivided interest in property, without the right of survivorship.

Testate: Dying with a will.

Testator: A person who has made a will or given a legacy.

Trust Amendment Form: A document that changes specific provisions of a revocable living trust but leaves all of the other provisions unchanged.

Trustee: An individual or firm that holds and administers property or assets for the benefit of a third party.

Unified Credit: Tax credit given to each individual upon death to be applied against estate tax owed.

Unlimited Marital Deduction: A provision allowing for the unrestricted transfer of assets from one spouse to the surviving spouse, free from tax.

Valuation Date: The date on which the value of an asset is determined for estate tax purposes.

Vesting: The process by which an employee with a qualified retirement plan and/or stock option becomes entitled to the benefits of ownership, even if the employee stops working with the company.

Ward: A person, usually a minor, who has a guardian appointed by the court to care for and take responsibility for that person (who is incapable of caring for his or her own affairs).

Will: A legal document that expresses a person's wishes as to how their property is to be distributed after their death and with which people (the executors) are to manage the property until its final distribution.

A Parting Gift

As a way of saying thank you for your purchase, we're offering two FREE downloads that are exclusive to our book readers!

First, the Estate Planning Checklist which shows you a step-by-step guide to getting your estate plan in order. Second, the Legacy Planning Workbook, which provides a roadmap for preserving your legacy and leaving a lasting impact on future generations. Inside these bonuses, **you'll discover:**

- An exact checklist for each phase of the estate planning process, so you leave no stone unturned and make sure you're fully prepared.
- A blueprint for sharing your values and having important conversations with heirs about your estate plan, so your wishes are properly fulfilled.
- The 6 key things you MUST have in order to properly preserve your legacy and leave your heirs protected.

To download your bonuses, you can go to **MonroeMethod.com/estate-plan or simply scan the QR code below:**

Can You Do Us a Favor?

Thanks for checking out our book.

We're confident this will help you plan your estate, protect your heirs, and leave a lasting legacy!

Would you take 60 seconds and write a quick blurb about this book on Amazon?

Reviews are the best way for independent authors (like us) to get noticed, sell more books, and spread our message to as many people as possible. We also read every review and use the feedback to write future revisions – and future books, even.

Just navigate to the link below or scan the QR code:

mybook.to/estate-planning

Thank you – we really appreciate your support.

About the Author

Garrett Monroe is a pen name for a team of writers with experience in various industries, like retirement planning, estate planning, entrepreneurship, sales, AI, real estate, accounting, etc. They've built teams, gone through the ins and outs of retirement, and know how to properly plan an estate. These writers have come together to share their knowledge and produce a series of books to help you retire well, plan your estate, and protect your loved ones for generations to come.

Citations

1. (n.d.). What Is a Legal Trust? Common Purposes, Types, and Structures. Investopedia. https://www.investopedia.com/terms/t/trust.asp

2. n.d.). Why Estate Planners Aren't Just For The Ultra-Rich. Forbes. https://www.forbes.com/sites/forbesfinancecouncil/2019/04/15/why-estate-planners-arent-just-for-the-ultra-rich/

3. n.d.). Generational Wealth: Overview, Examples and FAQs. Investopedia. https://www.investopedia.com/generational-wealth-definition-5189580

4. (n.d.). What you need to know about estate planning. LegalZoom. https://www.legalzoom.com/articles/what-you-need-to-know-about-estate-planning

5. (n.d.). What Does an Average Estate Plan Cost? (Detailed Price Analysis). FindLaw. https://www.findlaw.com/estate/planning-an-estate/what-does-an-average-estate-plan-cost-detailed-price-analysis.html

6. (n.d.). Negotiating Your Lawyers Hourly Fee. LegalMatch. https://www.legalmatch.com/law-library/article/negotiating-your-lawyers-hourly-fee.html

7. (n.d.). What Is a Trust Fund? The Balance Money. https://www.thebalancemoney.com/what-is-a-trust-fund-357254

8. Smith, L. (n.d.). What Is a Revocable Living Trust? Smart Asset. https://smartasset.com/retirement/what-is-a-revocable-living-trust

9. Nirenstein, J. A. (n.d.). 5 Reasons Wills Aren't A Sufficient Estate Plan. Preserve Your Estate.

https://preserveyourestate.net/blog/wills-and-trusts/5-reasons-wills-arent-sufficient-estate-plan/

10. (n.d.). What Is a Pension? Types of Plans and Taxation. Investopedia. https://www.investopedia.com/terms/p/pensionplan.asp

11. (n.d.). Inherited IRA Rules & SECURE Act 2.0 Changes. Charles Schwab. https://www.schwab.com/learn/story/inherited-ira-rules-secure-act-20-changes

12. Chubb, C. (n.d.). 2021 Estate Planning Checkup: Is Your Estate Plan Up to Date? Kiplinger. https://www.kiplinger.com/retirement/estate-planning/603199/2021-estate-planning-checkup-is-your-estate-plan-up-to-date

13. Kagan, J. (n.d.). Probate: What It Is and How It Works With and Without a Will. Investopedia. https://www.investopedia.com/terms/p/probate.asp

14. Beiber, C. (n.d.). How To Avoid Probate In 2024. Forbes. https://www.forbes.com/advisor/legal/estate-law/how-avoid-probate/

15. Bailey, M. (n.d.). Just Get Started! Overcoming Procrastination and Fear In Setting Up Your Estate Plan. Michael Bailey Law LLC. https://michaelbaileylawllc.com/just-get-started-overcoming-procrastination-and-fear-in-setting-up-your-estate-plan/